Meditations from the Oratory

EXPERIENCING
the MYSTERY
of CHRIST

Meditations from the Oratory

EXPERIENCING *the* MYSTERY *of* CHRIST

Fr. Benedict J. Groeschel, C.F.R.
Gerard and Yolanda Cleffi

Our Sunday Visitor Publishing Division
Our Sunday Visitor, Inc.
Huntington, Indiana 46750

He (Jesus) prays for us, he prays in us, and he is prayed to by us. He prays for us as our priest; he prays in us as our head; and he is prayed to by us as our God. Let us therefore recognize our voices in him and his voices in us.

— St. Augustine
(*Enarratio in Psalmum*, 85: CCL 39, 1176)

Contents

Preface

This second volume of *Meditations from the Oratory* has been a long time in coming. When I had just gotten through Meditation Twelve of this volume, I was struck by a car and had a long period of recuperation. Jerry and Yolanda Cleffi very generously and spontaneously took on the responsibility of writing the meditations for the Oratory. I am deeply grateful to them for that because their work kept the Oratory of Divine Love alive. The Oratory, as you may know, is a movement of people — devout people — who meet every week or every other week in their homes to meditate on Scripture and pray together.

We decided several years ago to publish these meditations in book form with the help of Michael Dubruiel at Our Sunday Visitor. I am grateful that the Cleffis undertook to write the rest of the meditations in this book. I have reviewed all of them and find them to contain solid Catholic teaching and to be very helpful and inspirational. The Cleffis are converts to the Church. Before their conversion, they served for some years as ministers in the Assemblies of God. Both of them hold master's degrees in theology from Saint Joseph's Seminary in New York. I am also

9

deeply indebted to John Collins, who has carefully edited the manuscript, as well as to Fr. Peter De Sanctis, Fr. Carleton Jones, O.P., and Alice Petro for their comments and criticisms.

We hope that you will enjoy this new volume and profit by it. It can be used for personal reading as well as for meetings of friends. Please, if you are having meetings of friends, be in touch with us at the address of the Oratory of Divine Love. This movement, begun by St. Catherine of Genoa, quietly laid the foundation for the reform of the Church in very troubled times — times not so different from the ones we live in.

What you can be sure of is that I pray every day at Mass for all of the members of the Oratory as well as for all who spiritually profit from any of our books. I hope and trust that you will pray for us.

Sincerely in Christ,
Fr. Benedict J. Groeschel, C.F.R.
Conversion of St. Paul, January 25, 2008

Introduction

This book is the second of four volumes outlining prayer meetings for devout Catholics. It contains weekly meditations first composed for prayer groups who wished to meditate and pray together on the truths of the Catholic faith. The first of such groups in history, made up of devout informed laity, goes back to the late fifteenth century, which was a time of great turmoil and scandal in the Church. A number of priests and people, under the inspiration of St. Catherine of Genoa (1447–1510), banded together to study the Bible and Church teachings, joining their study to a life of serious prayer and good works. A laywoman known as Caterinetta Fieschi Adorna, St. Catherine was director of the Pammatone in Genoa, the largest charity hospital in the world. She and her spiritual followers called the first prayer groups Oratories of Divine Love. The Italian word for prayer group is *oratorio*, which in turn is derived from the Latin word for prayer, *oratio*.

The Oratory of Divine Love was revived in America at the beginning of the new millennium as part of an effort by the Franciscan Friars of the Renewal to encourage Church reform. Although these meditations were written specifically for the Oratory, the simple outline and structure are not restricted to the Oratory or its members. We hope that they will be helpful to all who wish to grow in their faith and in the love of God and neighbor. Any group of devout people can grow and learn using these meditations, whether at weekly meetings or on their own.

Members of the Oratory today, as in the past, bind themselves to lead a devout life, to reverent participation in the liturgy, and to virtuous works of charity and religion. Oratorians still take on good works; for example, helping out at soup kitchens and other works for the needy, visiting the sick and homebound, and regular friendly visits to the elderly. Today, works of religion can include pro-life activities; assisting in a parish, especially in religious education; or being a Eucharistic minister to the homebound.

These books of Oratory meditations are being published one volume each year over the course of four years to make a complete cycle of Catholic faith and Scripture. When complete, each of the books will correspond to one of the four parts of the *Catechism of the Catholic Church*:

Book I. The Profession of Faith
Book II. The Celebration of the Christian Mystery
Book III. Life in Christ
Book IV. Christian Prayer

So, as Book I, *Praying with the Creed*, examined the truths of the Catholic faith as outlined in the Creed, this book moves us on to the second phase of our prayer journey: the consideration of the sacraments and liturgy — that is, Christ's work in union with the Holy Spirit to bring the blessings of the heavenly Father into our lives and world. It will be helpful for readers of these books to have on hand a copy of the *Catechism*, with which they will become familiar.

Those who meet only sporadically should try to cover each of the meditations given here, even if on their own. It is advisable to limit meetings to an hour, or perhaps an hour and a half, to avoid tedium. It is important to keep in mind that the overall plan for this series is to follow the *Catechism* with its four major divisions.

The original Oratories selected a reader who served for six months and coordinated the meeting. A group may also suggest someone as a permanent secretary, who corresponds with a central Oratory and tends to simple business matters, such as where meetings will be held, and circulates information about sick or needy members. It is intended that the structure and operations of the Oratory be very simple.

Whether you belong to the Oratory or not, we hope that you will find this book spiritually beneficial. Further, we hope that the serious study of the Scriptures and the Catholic faith will make you a deeper witness to the saving grace of Our Lord Jesus Christ and an active participant in the work of reform of the Church. Reform is just beginning and can be seen particularly in the young people known as the John Paul II generation. There is much to do, as Pope Benedict XVI has indicated: the restoration of a sense of awe and reverence; the renewal of Catholic education, which is often mediocre when not positively destructive; the strengthening of the priesthood with the resurrection of religious life; and the work of loving care for the poor and unfortunate.

Don't think of the prayer groups as a small beginning. Professor John Olin, a distinguished historian, has written:

> Sometime between 1514 and 1517 a branch of this Oratory was established in Rome — an event which Pastor and other historians have singled out as marking the beginning of effective Catholic reform in this troubled age.[1]

———

There is a serious movement in the diocese of Genoa at the present time to propose St. Catherine as a Doctor of the Church. This initiative has been strengthened by the interest of former archbishops of Genoa Tarcisio Cardinal Bertone, S.D.B., who is now papal secretary of state, and the late Giuseppe Cardinal Siri. Were Catherine so honored, she would be the first married laywoman to receive that title. We Oratorians hope that she will be so recognized because her spiritual teachings, particularly her doctrine on purgatory, have deeply affected the Catholic Church for several centuries. We hope that you will read about St. Catherine and get to know this remarkable person, who can be said to have begun the Catholic Reformation. Her mystical teachings on purgatory presenting this belief positively as a motive for gratitude, hope, and love are most refreshing and encouraging. Her profound influence on the Protestant Holiness movement in the nineteenth century is a remarkable chapter in ecumenical relations. Any serious Christian will be deeply moved by her spiritual writings and her life.[2]

In the meantime, your participation in the weekly Oratory meditations may prove spiritually beneficial to you or to your group. If they do, we would be grateful to hear from you at the Oratory:

Oratory of Divine Love
P.O. Box 1465
Bloomfield, NJ 07003

Meditation One

The Experience of the
Mystery of Christy

The Experience of the Mystery of Christ

✒︎

READINGS
*Ephesians 1:3–10; 3:1–9; Romans 16:25–27; Colossians 1:24–27;
Mark 4:11; Luke 8:10;* Catechism *1061–1068*

The idea of mystery is essential to any real appreciation of the Christian faith. Our Lord speaks of the mysteries of the kingdom of God (Lk 8:10), and St. Paul writes of the mysteries of Christ (Rom 16:25–27). The Apostle also tells us in dramatic language of the depth of the riches and knowledge of God and "how unsearchable are his judgments and how inscrutable his ways" (Rom 11:33). Apart from the direct effects of original sin — pride, irreverence, and self-love (often called narcissism) — it can be said that the greatest spiritual and religious calamities of modern times are traceable to the rejection of the experience of mystery.

Our ancestors lived in times when the operation of the physical world seemed profoundly mysterious. Over the centuries, however, science has pushed back the borders of mystery so that many things, once mysterious and unknown, are now well-understood. However, anyone with a deep understanding of science is aware that despite all that we have discovered about the working of the universe, great mysteries still surround us. Each major scientific breakthrough brings to light new knowledge, but it also reveals another layer of mystery. The origin of the universe (the big bang theory), the nature of matter, gravity, light, and life itself are all wrapped in great mystery. Superficial scientific presentations, the type we usually see in the media, simply ignore such great mysteries.

In complete contrast to this superficiality, Albert Einstein, considered by many the greatest scientist who ever lived, wrote:

> The most beautiful and most profound emotion we can experience is the sensation of the mystical. It is the sower of all true science. He to whom this emotion is a stranger, who can no longer wonder and stand rapt in awe, is as good as dead. To know that what is impenetrable to us really exists, manifesting itself as the highest wisdom and the most radiant beauty which our dull faculties can comprehend only in their most primitive

forms — this knowledge, this feeling is at the center of true religiousness.[3]

The liturgy, the sacraments, and grace itself are all profoundly mysterious, but they are supernatural rather than natural mysteries. To give a superficial explanation of gravity, matter, or physical life may be stupid, but it's nothing compared to explaining away Christ or His gifts of grace conferred by the sacraments or His mysterious words in the Gospel. Much that is written now about Christ, the sacraments, the Church, and even about Scripture, lacks an adequate sense of mystery as Einstein defines it. Therefore, such writing often ends up being superficial, false, or even heretical. Several priests, some of them still alive, have reported that Einstein was fascinated by the Catholic dogma of the Holy Eucharist, a substance with no appearances of its real nature. It should surprise no one that a man so sensitive to the mysterious should be attracted to the mystery of all mysteries.

We would all do better if we had a greater sense of mystery. Just as the mystery of the origin of the universe is the greatest of scientific mysteries, so the Paschal Mystery, including the events of Our Savior's life from the Incarnation to the Ascension and His Second Coming, comprise the great mystery of our faith. The Paschal Mystery focuses on Christ's sacrificial death and Resurrection and is of the greatest possible importance to us, for it tells us how we will be saved and enter everlasting life. In the meditations that follow, we will look at the liturgy, a word that describes all the mysterious actions centering on Baptism and the Holy Eucharist, which unite us with Christ, our only salvation.

Quotation for Meditation

"The wonderful works of God among the people of the Old Testament were but a prelude to the work of Christ the Lord in redeeming mankind and giving perfect glory to God. He accomplished this work principally by the Paschal mystery of His blessed Passion, Resurrection from the dead, and glorious Ascension, whereby 'dying He destroyed our death, rising He restored our life.' For it was from the side of Christ as he slept the sleep of death upon the cross that there came forth 'the wondrous sacrament of the whole Church.'" For this reason the Church celebrates in the liturgy above all the Paschal mystery, by which Christ accomplished the work of our salvation.

It is this mystery of Christ that the Church proclaims and celebrates in her liturgy so that the faithful may live from it and bear witness to it in the world:

> For it is in the liturgy, especially in the divine sacrifice of the Eucharist, that "the work of our redemption is accomplished," and it is through the liturgy especially

that the faithful are enabled to express in their lives and manifest to others the mystery of Christ and the real nature of the true Church.

— *Catechism of the Catholic Church*, 1067–1068

Quiet Time and Then Discussion

Questions for Meditation

1. Do I think sometimes of the mysteries that surround us in the physical world, like gravity, matter, and light?
2. Do I think reverently of the mysteries of God: creation, the body, and the soul?
3. Do I think of the mystery of Christ, His Divine Person, His human nature, His grace and glory, and the gift of salvation?

Prayer

Heavenly Father, Your Being and nature are completely beyond my mind or any other human mind. I can only fall in adoration of Your Being and Your decision to know each of Your children and call us to Your eternal home.

Lord Jesus Christ, how can I ever embrace all that Your mysterious Being means to us? You are the Son of the Eternal Father, and yet mysteriously You are brother to us poor mortals. And You work for our salvation through the sacraments and liturgy as well as Your Holy Gospel.

Open our hearts and minds to Your mystery, O Holy Spirit, Spirit of divine mercy. Come into our hearts and be our inner teacher so that we may fall in adoration of the divine mysteries, that we may penetrate them as far as we can, and accept with joy and gratitude what our minds cannot grasp. Amen.

Meditation Two

The Liturgy of Christ

READINGS

John 15:1–11; Ephesians 2:4–10; 3:14–19; Galatians 2:20;
Catechism *1069–1074*

The word "liturgy" has numerous meanings. Most commonly it is a word used to indicate the Mass, but it means many things other than that and therefore can become confusing. Liturgy includes all the works that Christ, our High Priest, does in His Church. In its broadest application, liturgy includes any exercise of Christ's own ministry as Head of the Mystical Body, the Church. This, of course, includes public worship, especially the celebration of the Holy Eucharist; but it also includes the other sacraments, other forms of worship, all good works done in union with Christ by His followers, all preaching and teaching of the Gospel, and all works of true charity. The liturgy joins the action and blessing of the Son of God to the works of human beings.

Interestingly, liturgy does not include all actions of Christians. Such things as coming to faith and conversion are not included, for these are things that precede the work of Christ and prepare for them even though Christ's grace operates through these works. So we understand that although personal conversion and repentance are not part of the liturgy of Christ, His grace alone makes them happen. His grace opens us to His liturgy. When we work for the conversion of others, however, that is liturgy because it is a work of Christ. It requires a degree of maturity and spiritual insight to realize that the whole work of salvation and sanctification, the whole reason for our being Christians, is to allow the Son of God to grow in us so that we may be transformed into Him. He alone has eternal life, and our entrance into that life depends on our incorporation into Him.

As we begin this consideration of the second section of the *Catechism*, we must be clear that we are not simply studying religious services, the liturgy of the Mass, or the sacraments as the externals of our great world religion. We are meditating on the mysterious operation in our world of the Son of God, Jesus our eternal High Priest. "I am with you always, to the close of the age" (Mt 28:20), Jesus said. How much these words mean when we study them in this context:

Quotation for Meditation

The word "liturgy" originally meant a "public work" or a "service in the name of/on behalf of the people." In Christian tradition it means the participation of the People of God in "the work of God."[4] Through the liturgy Christ, our redeemer and high priest, continues the work of our redemption in, with, and through his Church.

In the New Testament the word "liturgy" refers not only to the celebration of divine worship but also to the proclamation of the Gospel and to active charity.[5] In all of these situations it is a question of the service of God and neighbor. In a liturgical celebration the Church is servant in the image of her Lord, the one *leitourgos*; she shares in Christ's priesthood (worship), which is both prophetic (proclamation) and kingly (service of charity):

> The liturgy then is rightly seen as an exercise of the priestly office of Jesus Christ. It involves the presentation of man's sanctification under the guise of signs perceptible by the senses and its accomplishment in ways appropriate to each of these signs. In it full public worship is performed by the Mystical Body of Jesus Christ, that is, by the Head and his members. From this it follows that every liturgical celebration, because it is an action of Christ the priest and of his body which is the

Church, is a sacred action surpassing all others. No other action of the Church can equal its efficacy by the same title and to the same degree.

— *Catechism of the Catholic Church*, 1069, 1070

◈ Quiet Time and Then Discussion ◈

Questions for Meditation

1. Do I ever think of my real life in this world as Christ living and acting in me? This is the real meaning of grace.
2. Do I see Christ in my mind when I participate in the Eucharist and the other sacraments?
3. Do I show the reverence that Christ's presence and action should inspire in us?

Prayer

Lord Jesus Christ, how many times I have been in touch with Your presence, Your ministry to myself and to others. I pray that the Holy Spirit will waken me from my slumber and distraction so that I may rejoice in Your work in my soul and in the souls of others. Let me come to know You every day in Your work as Savior. Amen.

The Sacramental Dispensation of Grace

⸙

READINGS
John 3:10–18; Ephesians 1:3–10; Hebrews 4:14–16; 5:5–10;
Catechism *1076–1085*

In recent decades there has been a regrettable loss of the sense of God's grace in our lives. There is also a great decline in appreciating the sacraments as a source of such grace. If people think of grace at all, they are likely to consider it a religious experience, a sense of God's presence in the individual soul. Certainly such an experience can and should be a reflection of God's grace in our lives, but it is not grace itself. Grace cannot be restricted to mere religious experience. In fact, to do so is dangerous. There are some holy souls, like Mother Teresa, who suffer the feeling of God's absence, enduring a constant thirst for Him. This too is a grace and is known as the dark night of the soul. It certainly doesn't feel like a grace, but it is.

There are people today who claim they experience the divine presence in various New Age rituals. This, however, is false. Such rituals merely induce a psychological state brought on by the conscious control of various neurological factors (called alpha rhythms). In the scriptural sense this has nothing to do with grace, although God could certainly use it. Such a state resembles the uplifting feeling one can have listening to Handel's *Messiah* or some other great work of music. It is certainly a pleasant state, but it is not grace. We must also be aware that the potential for harm exists in some New Age activities. Experiences of a sinister presence have been reported in the rituals of Wicca, a form of modern paganism. This is either self-hypnosis or, far more dangerous, the actual effect of an evil spirit. For this reason every Christian must avoid and denounce any form of natural religiosity as a substitute for Christian prayer. These things are simply violations of the first commandment. Wicca and all the nonsense associated with it may not be just ridiculous; they may be diabolical.

The opposite of a subjective experience of grace, whether authentic, imagined, or sinister, is God's plan of salvation. This is our redemption by Christ's suffering, the washing away of sin by His holy blood, and our incorporation into His life, especially by the sacraments, which He left to the Church to distribute.

Because of a lack of adequate instruction concerning God's plan of salvation, we need to take time to meditate on this subject. This aspect of Christ's work of salvation is called the plan of the sacraments or, to use the theological term, the economy of the sacraments. "Economy" in this sense has nothing to do with money or financial concerns, as it is usually does. Here it means the mysterious plan of God, by which Christ has saved us from eternal loss through the mercy of the Father. Christ has done this by His holy human life, which made Him — although utterly sinless Himself — vulnerable to the sins of the world and the evil plans of Satan. His divine love for His Father caused Christ to accept death on the Cross as a sacrificial offering. He forgave His enemies and all the sins of the world by His loving obedience in life and especially in His holy, but terrible, death. He became the Lamb of God who takes away the sins of the world. Although Christ has ascended into heaven, He continues to work in the world as Savior through His word in the Gospels and the rest of the New Testament and through His sacraments.

As we examine the sacraments, we will see that it is Christ who baptizes, absolves sin, anoints, blesses, and continues the Church, which is His own Mystical Body. As we study the Church's worship and the sacraments that are given to us by Christ, let us grow in appreciation of and gratitude for all that our Divine Savior has done for us.

Quotation for Meditation

God our Savior planned to recall man from the fall. Man's disobedience separated him from God's household, and God wished to bring him back. This is why Christ took flesh, and accomplished everything described in the Gospels: His sufferings, the cross, the tomb, the resurrection, so that man might be saved through imitation of Christ and receive his original birthright. If we are to be perfect, we must not only imitate Christ's meekness, humility, and long-suffering, but His death as well. Paul surely was an imitator of Christ, and he says, "that I may know him and the power of his resurrection, and may share his sufferings, becoming like him in his death, that if possible I may attain the resurrection from the dead" (Phil 3:10–11). How can we become like Him in His death? By being buried with Him in baptism (Rom 6:4–5). What kind of burial is it, and what is gained from such imitation? First, it is necessary that the old way of life be terminated, and this is impossible unless a man is born again, as the Lord has said (Jn 3:3). Regeneration, as its very name reveals, is a beginning of a second life. Before beginning a second life, one must put an end to the first. When a runner has to run around the post at the end of the racetrack in order to return on the other side of the course, he has to stop and pause momentarily, in order to negotiate such a sharp turn. So also if we are going to change our lives, death must come between what has already happened (ending it) and what is just beginning. How can we accomplish this descent into death? By imitating the burial of Christ through baptism. The bodies of those being baptized are buried in the water. Thus baptism signifies the putting off of the works of the flesh.

— *St. Basil on the Holy Spirit*

Quiet Time and Then Discussion

Questions for Meditation

1. Do I think of God's great plan of redemption, or am I simply following my own religious experience?
2. Do I speak to others about Christ's work as our Savior?
3. Do I speak up kindly but directly when I see examples of superstition and the occult occurring in the name of religion?

Prayer

Jesus, my Savior, all my life I have thought of You as my Savior. But have I perceived the meaning of this great mystery? Have I recognized that Your Passion and sacrifice have purchased salvation for me and those I love? Give me the gift of Your Holy Spirit in abundance so that in every-day life I may be Your true disciple and witness to the mysteries of salvation accomplished by Your death and Resurrection. Amen.

The Meaning of the Sacraments

∿

READINGS

Baptism — *Matthew 28:19; Mark 16:16; John 3:5*
Eucharist — *Luke 22:14–22; John 6:47–51*
Apostles — *Acts 2:37–47; 1 Corinthians 11:23–29;*
Catechism *1086–1089*

Until a few decades ago, every Catholic child knew that "a sacrament was an outward sign instituted by Christ to give grace." This was a very good thing to know, although it was a bit oversimplified. It is time for us now to look more deeply at these wellsprings of divine grace, to understand their source and their meaning in God's plan of salvation for us.

The scriptural foundations of the sacraments are most obvious in regards to Baptism and the Holy Eucharist. No one can read the Gospels without realizing that Christ explicitly commanded His Apostles to baptize and to celebrate the Eucharist. He clearly taught the necessity of both these sacraments as can be

seen in the texts cited above. The bases in the Gospels of some of
the other sacraments are more subtle, but they become more
explicit in the writings of St. James and St. Paul. This is true in
the case of the Anointing of the Sick and of Matrimony. The
Church's teaching on these two sacraments comes out of Christ's
healing of the sick and His ordering the Apostles to heal others
by laying hands on them (Mk 16:18). It is also founded on His
presence at the marriage feast of Cana, and His teaching on marriage (Jn 2:1–11). For these reasons they have always been
included among the liturgical sacraments.

Protestant churches have varying numbers of rites that they
call sacraments. Often they give meanings to them that are different from the Catholic understanding of a sacrament. The
Orthodox, as well as the very ancient churches of the East —
often referred to as Apostolic or Oriental Churches — all celebrate the same seven sacraments we do. They do so in a manner
and with an understanding so similar to ours that the Catholic
Church readily recognizes the validity of their sacraments.

Just as Christ was sent by the Father through the Holy Spirit
to save the fallen human race, so Our Savior sent the Apostles,
filled with the Holy Spirit, to bring the Good News to the ends
of the earth. But as we know so well, the Apostles were just weak
mortal men, very capable of betraying the Lord in His hour of
need. They could not save anybody on their own. He had to be

with them, and He promised He would be, even to the end of the world. The means by which Christ's life and presence remain with His Church are called the divine mysteries by the Eastern Church Fathers and sacraments by the Western Church Fathers. A sacrament in this sense is a promise of grace, and Christ alone is the source of grace. The early Church was very aware that Christ is present and acting in every sacrament. That is why St. Augustine reminds us in the readings below that the worthiness of the minister does not affect the power of the sacrament — because it is Christ who gives the sacraments. We should respond to this by receiving every sacrament with the greatest reverence. If we are prayerfully attentive, we will experience His presence in the sacraments.

In our church in the South Bronx, we have regular Eucharistic adoration, and elderly African American ladies who live in the neighborhood come to pray before the Blessed Sacrament. Although they belong to little storefront churches — often of denominations founded by freed slaves who in their fervent love for Christ saw Him as a fellow victim — these ladies will say: "Go into that church, and the sweet Lord Jesus is there. You can tell. You can feel Him." How wonderful it would be if we all had the same reverence.

Quotations for Meditation

"The reason these things, brothers and sisters, are called sacraments is that in them one thing is seen, another is to be understood. What can be seen has a bodily appearance, what is to be understood provides spiritual fruit."

———

"I have entrusted you with something sacramental which, when spiritually understood, will give you life. Although it must of necessity be celebrated in visible form, it must still be understood invisibly."

———

"This power of faith has so much power in the Church of God that through the very one who believes, offers, blesses, immerses, it cleanses even the tiny infant, not yet having the capacity with its heart to believe to justice and with its mouth to make a profession of faith to salvation. All this is done through the word, of which the Lord says: 'Now you are clean by reason of the word that I have spoken to you.'"

———

"But men put on Christ, sometimes so far as to receive the sacrament, sometimes so much further as to receive holiness of life. And the first of these is common to good and bad alike; the second, peculiar to the good and pious."

———

"But the baptism of Christ, consecrated by the words of the Gospel, is necessarily holy, however polluted and unclean its ministers may be; because its inherent sanctity cannot be polluted, and the divine excellence abides in its sacrament, whether to the salvation of those who use it right, or to the destruction of those who use it wrong."

———

"[T]hey whom a drunkard baptized, or those whom a murderer baptized, those whom an adulterer baptized, if it were the baptism of Christ, were baptized by Christ."

———

"Jesus, therefore, is still baptizing; and so long as we continue to be baptized, Jesus baptizes. Let a man come without fear to the minister below; for he has a Master above."

— As cited in Emmanuel J. Cutrone, "Sacraments,"
in *Augustine Through the Ages*, 745–746

≈ Quiet Time and Then Discussion ≈

Questions for Meditation

1. Do I realize and worship Christ's presence in the sacraments?
2. Do I show my loyalty and gratitude to Christ each day for my Baptism?
3. Do I give an example of profound reverence to Christ's presence in the Holy Eucharist?

Prayer

O Lord Jesus, You have come to be with our fallen race so that we may be saved. You have never left us. You are with us in the poor and suffering. We see Your presence as Word of God in the beauty of the sky and the earth. But most of all You are with us in the sacraments. Give us Your Holy Spirit that we may recognize and be glad in Your presence. Amen.

Meditation Five

The Liturgy:
A Foretaste of Heaven

READINGS
Hebrews 4:14–16; 5:5–10; 10:19–25; 12:1–4;
Revelation 19:1–9; 22:1–5; Catechism *1090*

Early on, the Church Fathers saw that the celebration of the Holy Eucharist was a preparation for and a mirror of the heavenly Jerusalem, our true and lasting home. While we can have in our mind no actual images of eternal life (what "eye has not seen"), it is also true that Christ's act of love in dying on the Cross for us as our sacrificial Paschal Lamb is the act of complete worship of the Holy Trinity. All who are saved by His blood are united to Him in this act of worship. In a certain sense the only action we do here on earth that is substantially the same as what we will do in heaven is the worship we offer to God in union with Christ. We are led in this worship by the Blessed Mother of Jesus, His first disciple and the one completely given to His service. We are joined by all the saints, who are redeemed and united with Christ and the angels. This union with Christ is made known in the Epistle to the Hebrews and in many writings of St. Paul. St. Paul sees eternal life beginning here on earth as we become members of the Mystical Body of Christ and Christ comes to dwell in us.

The Eucharistic sacrifice, which proclaims the death of the Lord until He comes, and the reception of the Bread of Life are the visible means of Christ's relationship with those He has saved by Baptism into His Blood. In the Latin Rite liturgy the celebration of the Last Supper is stressed; in the liturgy of the East, especially that of St. John Chrysostom, the heavenly liturgy to come is the primary focus. These differences do not affect the essential elements, but they do explain the relative simplicity of the Latin liturgy compared to the grandeur of the Eastern Rites. It is enlightening and enriching to be familiar with both liturgical forms. In the Latin Rite today, Mass may be celebrated according to two forms: the *Novus Ordo*, promulgated in 1969 and usually said in the vernacular; and the Tridentine usage, celebrated in Latin according to the 1962 Missal.

It is essential for us to recall where we are headed — to the heavenly city, to spend eternity in the company of the saints. From the earliest days of the Church, Christians have honored the saints not only as models for living the Christian life, but as their friends and representatives before the throne of God. The author of the letter to the Hebrews calls them a "cloud of wit-nesses." They are celebrated beautifully in the book of Revela-tion. When we attend Mass, we should know that they are present, as are the angels. They and all the members of the Mys-tical Body of Christ stand in the radiance of endless day. If we could but remember this, every Mass no matter how simply cel-ebrated would be overwhelmingly beautiful and awe-inspiring. How sad it is when we become oblivious of these truths, when the Mass becomes a habit, a chore, something to get done. We have eyes but do not see.

Quotation for Meditation

"By grace you have been saved through faith," said St. Paul, "not because of works, lest any man should boast" (Eph 2:8a, 9).

Who, then, merits all praise? To whom does the glory of our holiness return? To Christ Jesus.

When the Apostle sets the divine plan before the faithful of Ephesus, he indicates in these words the supreme end: God has thus preordained all things "unto the praise of the glory of His grace." Thus, "that He might show in the years to come the abun-dant riches of His grace," God has predestined us to become the co-heirs of His Son.

Here below, we owe all to Jesus; by His mysteries He has merited for us all the graces of justification, of forgiveness, of sanctification that we need: Christ is the very principle of our perfection. As the vine pours forth its nourishing sap into the branches so that they may bear fruit, so Christ Jesus ceaselessly pours forth His grace into all those who abide in Him. . . .

In heaven likewise all the glory of the saints is derived from this same grace; all the splendor of their triumph comes from this one source. It is because they are dyed with the blood of the Lamb that the garments of the elect shine so resplendently; and the degree of their holiness is measured by the degree of their likeness to the Divine Model. . . .

In heaven we shall comprehend that all God's mercies took their rise on Calvary. The blood of Jesus is the price of the heavenly happiness which we shall then forevermore enjoy. In the heavenly Jerusalem we shall be inebriated with divine gladness; but every instant of this joy will have been paid by the merits of the blood of Christ Jesus. The river of beatitude which eternally flows in this city of God has its source in the sacrifice of our divine High Priest. It will be an immense joy for us to acknowledge this and to sing our joy and praise and thanksgiving to Jesus.

Like the elect, we shall cast our crowns at His feet to testify that we owe them to Him. It is to this last end that all the mystery of Christ tends. God wills that His Son Jesus shall be forever exalted because He is His own Only-begotten Son, the object of His complacency; because this Son, although He was God, annihilated

Himself so as to sanctify His Mystical Body: "Therefore God has highly exalted Him."

Let us then enter with deep faith into these divine mysteries. When we celebrate the feasts of the saints, we magnify the power of the grace that has raised them to these summits; nothing is more well-pleasing to God, because by this praise we unite ourselves with the most intimate of His designs, which is to glorify His Son: "I have glorified it [my name], and I will glorify it again." Let us ourselves seek to realize, with the help of this same grace, the design of God for each one of us; yet once more it is in this perfect conformity that all holiness is summed up.

— Blessed Columba Marmion,
Christ in His Mysteries, Chapter 20

☙ Quiet Time and Then Discussion ❧

Questions for Meditation

1. In the midst of life's struggles, do I sometimes stop to think of heaven, the place where Christ has called us?

2. When I am at Mass, do I think of the heavenly realities around me, or am I just distracted?

3. Do I encourage others to pray silently before, during, and after Mass, at least by prayerful example?

Prayer

Lord Jesus Christ, You are always a merciful Savior, a friend when no one else is there. You are the one who has suffered so much for me. Give me Your Holy Spirit so that my heart may rise to some awareness of Your heavenly priesthood. Help me to remind others that this is the destiny we are called to if only we follow You. Help me to seek first the kingdom of heaven. Amen.

Meditation Six

The Holy Spirit and the Liturgy

READINGS
John 14:25–31; 15:26–27; 16:1–15;
Catechism *1091–1103*

It is most unfortunate that despite the great effort to make the liturgy and the sacraments more meaningful to the clergy and the faithful since Vatican II, much of the result seems to be superficial. Great attention can be paid on all sides to the less important aspects of the Mass and the rest of the Church's liturgy. Arguments rage about who should assist, what language should be used, what hymns should be sung, what to wear, and when to kneel and stand. All these things are of some importance, but it seems that the most important elements are overlooked. This is especially true when it concerns the presence and work of the Holy Spirit in the liturgy. Most people could not tell you what the Holy Spirit has to do with the sacraments, although they could tell you that Christ's presence and action are important.

In order to have a deep appreciation of the reason that Christ promises at the Last Supper to send the Holy Spirit to the Church, we must meditate on chapters 14 to 16 of St. John's Gospel, especially the texts indicated above. The *Catechism* describes the works of the Holy Spirit, and if you examine your own prayer life, you may notice that the Spirit has been doing His work in you all along but you did not realize it. When it comes to prayer in union with Christ, the Holy Spirit helps us in the following ways.

1.   He prepares us by inspiring us to pray and learn from the Bible — the New Testament, of course, but also the Jewish Scriptures, or the Old Testament, and especially the book of Psalms. He opens our minds to the meaning of the figures or signs of the Old Testament like the Exodus (Baptism), the Paschal Lamb (the sacrifice of the Eucharist), the manna (reception of the Bread of Life). There are many figures, like the Ark of the Covenant, that point to the coming of Christ and His salvation of mankind. In a Benedictine abbey in California there is a tabernacle built as a replica of the Ark.

2.   The Holy Spirit brings to mind the whole mystery of Christ. This is essential since the liturgy is a memorial of the mystery of salvation. Always take a few minutes

before Mass to pray deeply to the Holy Spirit. In that short time and with His help, the whole mystery of Christ can pass before our minds. This is known as the anamnesis, or the recalling in faith of the mystery of salvation. It takes place at the beginning of Mass. As we prepare for Mass, we need to take time to pray and recall what we are doing. We must allow the Holy Spirit to do what Christ says He will do: "[He will] bring to your remembrance all that I have said to you" (Jn 14:26).

In our next meditation we will continue with the two other works of the Holy Spirit — how He actually causes the sacrament to come into being and how He gives us Communion, not only for ourselves but for the whole Church.

Quotation for Meditation

When Christ for the last time, shortly before His death, assembled His disciples, He spoke to them thus: "But the Paraclete, the Holy Spirit, whom the Father will send in my name, He will teach you all things, and brings all things to your mind, whatsoever I shall have said to you."

It is impossible to understand and accept Christ in the manner in which we understand and accept other historical figures. In Him the Son of God has become man and dwells among us.

This is a mystery so profound that it surpasses the power of our intellect; it is also a judgment on the world which forces us to change our entire mode of thinking and reassess all our values.

Unaided, we cannot understand Christ. The faculty of understanding can be awakened only by the One who is Christ's equal — the Holy Spirit through whose power the Son of God became man. The Holy Spirit opens the heart and the mind, and our prayer to Him is the prayer by which we ask that we may understand Christ.

As a historical figure, Christ is easily blurred by similarity with other historical figures, and also by the fact that man has an instinctive aversion to anything which goes beyond the purely human. The Holy Spirit must grant us the gift of discrimination. The figure of Christ, as well as His message, is surrounded by misunderstandings, distortions, and hostility.

The Holy Spirit must give assurance to our hearts and minds so that we may find the way to Him. Christ is the truth. The Holy Spirit must give this understanding of Christ, which in the words of St. Paul "surpasses everything," and must awaken our love for Him.

The Holy Spirit teaches us to understand Christ, and in Christ, God and ourselves. It is the kind of understanding which comes from the heart, not from the intellect. It is true comprehension; more than that, it is illumination.

The Holy Spirit gives us the answers to those questions which the mind cannot answer because the mind invariably couples the word why with the word I. "Why must I endure this suffering?" "Why am I denied what others have?" "Why must I be the way I am, live the way I do?" These are some of the most essential and decisive questions in the life of the individual, and to those questions men and books remain silent. The true answer comes only when our heart is free from revolt and bitterness; when our will has come to terms with life as it is for us, recognizing in it the working of the will of God.

The intellect may acquiesce readily enough, but this is not sufficient. Instruction must go deeper; acceptance must come from our inmost heart. Only then will we find the answer to the why, and with it, peace, for truth alone brings peace. This is the work of the Holy Spirit.

— Romano Guardini, *Prayer in Practice*, 93–95

❧ Quiet Time and Then Discussion ❧

Questions for Meditation

1. Do I pray to the Holy Spirit, asking Him to prepare me for Mass and the sacraments?

2. Do I read the Bible, especially the Psalms and the Gospels, to help me pray with Christ?
3. Do I encourage others to pray to the Holy Spirit so as to meet Christ in the Mass?

Prayer

Holy Spirit, open my mind and heart so that I may pray with Christ. Help me to know how to pray with Him. And Holy Spirit, pray within me so that I may pray well. Amen.

Meditation Seven

The Holy Spirit Makes the Mystery of Christ Present

~

READINGS
*John 6:41–51; 1 Corinthians 11:23–29; Ephesians 1:11–14;
2 Corinthians 1:19–22;* Catechism *1104–1112*

When we consider the Holy Eucharist and all the other sacraments, we are inclined to begin with the human side of things, because that is where we are. We think of the reception of the sacraments and the ceremonies that surround them. For this meditation, let's try to look at these mysteries from the other side, beginning with God, who in His great love for us, invites us to share in His eternal life through the sacraments. To suggest that we start by thinking of God's side of things may seem unrealistic, but it is, in fact, a great reality. We did not first love God; He first loved us and called us to Himself by His Divine Word, His own Son, in whom are all the treasures of wisdom and knowledge; and it is God who seals us with His Holy Spirit.

THE HOLY SPIRIT MAKES THE MYSTERY
OF CHRIST PRESENT

Out of all eternity comes the Word of God, who in His Incarnation is called Jesus, the Christ. He is truly God and truly man, and He calls us to salvation in every way possible. Humanly speaking, His mission on earth ended in absolute disaster and defeat, but He left behind His mysteries, the living remembrance of His love, and the sacramental signs of bread and wine. Based on the teaching found in John 6 and on St. Paul's teaching in 1 Corinthians 11, the Church has always understood the banquet of thanksgiving (Eucharist means thanksgiving) to be truly Christ's Body and Blood. No one really understands the way that this change of substance takes place. It is a mystery of God and will remain so. We do know, however, that the Holy Spirit is the cause of the transformation. What is most important is that God's Word, His Son, begins to live in us through Holy Communion and that this transforms us gradually into Christ, causing us to become more and more identified with Him.

To become one with Christ — or "to put on Christ Jesus," as St. Paul describes it — is our calling. This happens to us not only as individuals but also as members of the whole people of God, of the Church. We join Christ and His other members and form one body, a mystical, mysterious unity. Christ says that He is the vine and we are the branches, that we live in Him and the sap of life that unites us is the Holy Spirit. For this reason some have called the Church itself a sacrament. When we speak of "the

Church," we usually mean the visible reality, the parish, diocese, or the whole structure. The most important part of the Church, however, is the invisible part, the bond of divine grace, which unites the followers of Christ. This is the work of the Holy Spirit. He brings us communion, the sign of unity. St. Augustine calls it the chain of charity: *vinculum caritatis*.

It is important to try to grasp this unseen reality, which is contrary to our experience. We see the Church as a collection of individuals, some of whom we don't like and some of whom we disagree with. While it is not good to pretend that we all get along as one big happy family (we don't), it is necessary to work constantly for the sacramental unity that the Holy Eucharist causes and symbolizes. All this is accomplished not by our feeble efforts alone, but by the Holy Spirit. In the Epistle to the Hebrews (9:14), it says that Christ is led by the Eternal Spirit to offer His Blood to take away our sins. Do we really believe this?

Quotation for Meditation

The Holy Spirit is the source of truth and life-giving principle of the identity of the one, holy, catholic, and apostolic Church. The Holy Spirit is also the source and principle of the sacramental life through which the Church draws the strength of Christ, participates in his holiness, is nourished by his grace, and grows and advances on her journey toward eternity. The Holy Spirit, who is at the origin of the Incarnation of the Word, is the living source of all the sacraments instituted by Christ and at work in the Church. It is precisely through the sacraments that he gives people "new life," associating the Church to himself as his co-worker in this saving action . . . .

As for the Eucharist, in the New Testament its link with the Holy Spirit is marked more or less directly in the text of John's Gospel which recounts Jesus' announcement in the synagogue at Capernaum about the institution of the sacrament of his Body and Blood: "It is the Spirit which gives life, while the flesh is of no avail; the words I have spoken to you are spirit and life" (Jn 6:63). Both the word and the sacrament have life and operative effectiveness from the Holy Spirit.

Christian Tradition is aware of this bond between the Eucharist and the Holy Spirit which was expressed, and still is today, during the Mass when, in the epiclesis, the Church requests the sanctification of the gifts offered upon the altar: "by the power of your Spirit" (Eucharistic Prayer III); "let your Spirit come upon them" (Eucharistic Prayer II); "bless and approve our offering" (Eucharistic Prayer I). The Church emphasizes the mysterious power of the Holy Spirit for the completion of the Eucharistic consecration, for the sacramental transformation of bread and wine into the Body and Blood of Christ, and for the communication of grace to those who participate in it and to the entire Christian community.

— Pope John Paul II, *Dominum et Vivificantem*
(Lord and Giver of Life)

Quiet Time and Then Discussion

Questions for Meditation

1. We hear a lot of superficial talk about how the Eucharist brings us together, like people taking a meal together. Are we prepared to kindly open up to the same people the depth of the mystery of Holy Communion?
2. Do we think of and pray to the Holy Spirit when He unites us with Christ and each other?
3. Are we willing to acknowledge and embrace the mystery of our unity with Christ, even though it is a mystery?

Prayer

Holy Spirit, open our hearts and minds that we may fall in adoration before the reality of our union with Christ. You are there unseen to bring Christ to us in the mystery of His Body and Blood, and then to unite us with all souls in His Grace, that we may be united with Him. Despite the dullness of our minds, help us to be truly united with Him and all His members and to act as though we believe it. Amen.

Meditation Eight

The Sacraments and Eternal Life

READINGS
2 Peter 1:3–8; 1 Corinthians 11:23–27; Titus 2:11–14;
Catechism *1113–1134*

Our Lord instituted the sacraments to give the grace of His Paschal sacrifice to the members of His Mystical Body. The sacraments flow forth from the Church like streams of living water; their source is the whole body of Christ. This is not an easy idea to grasp, nor is it necessary to understand this concept fully in order to receive the sacraments devoutly. Nevertheless, it is a profound idea that can give us a deeper appreciation of our salvation.

Writing in the fifth century, St. Leo the Great said that sacraments are "powers that come forth from the Body of Christ." This is why it is proper for sacraments to be given always in union with the Church as the Body of Christ. However, in His great mercy, God has permitted some sacraments to be validly given to anyone trying to follow the way of Our Divine Savior. Therefore, Baptism, properly performed and with the right intention, is always valid. All Christians who enter a legitimate marriage receive the sacrament of matrimony; Catholics, however, are required to have the proper witness of a priest or deacon, unless no clergy can be present. The Church recognizes the validity of all the sacraments given in the Orthodox churches and, when necessary, provides pastoral authority for these sacraments, like Penance (or Reconciliation).

The basic rule on sacraments is that they are given by God for the salvation of souls and should not be restricted as long as the person who is to receive them has the correct disposition — sorrow for sin, a purpose of amendment, and the decision to give up sin and lead a good Christian life.

The reception of Holy Communion is a special sign of the Church's unity and requires membership in the Church. However, under certain circumstances members of the Orthodox churches can receive Communion at Mass, and under other circumstances we can receive the Eucharist at their liturgy with the approval of their clergy. Naturally, anyone going to Holy Communion must be united with us in our belief that the Eucharist is truly the Body and Blood of Christ.

It is very unfortunate that many in our times seem to be woefully ignorant of the meaning and holiness of the sacraments.

Following in the footsteps of the original Oratory of Divine Love, we should make a point of showing the greatest reverence for all the sacraments, especially the Holy Eucharist. Members of the Oratory are required to do good works of charity and of religion. A perfect work for our members is to become Eucharistic ministers for the sick and homebound and to fulfill this ministry with the greatest reverence. For example, we should remain silent and recollected when carrying the Holy Eucharist, and we must prepare appropriate prayers to be offered with the sick and their family members. It is a good idea for the Eucharistic minister to bring a small white linen cloth, on which to place the pyx, and two small vigil candles in order to emphasize the reverence due the Eucharist.

If an Oratorian is responsible for preparing someone for Baptism, the holy Anointing of the Sick, or for marriage, he or she should always do this in the most reverent way possible. We must wear our Sunday best and present at all times the attitude that the whole Church should have toward the sacraments: reverence and loving service of our Savior.

Quotation for Meditation

The Word came to be received by His people in human form. So humanly He continues His work of salvation among us, incarnate in things and men. Were it not so, we could not meet Him in a human way.

He continues this work in order to build up His Body. For through man's deification, through what he does, what he endures (suffering, death), that is the purpose of the sacramental economy. One flock, one Shepherd seeking His sheep through the ministers of His Word and of His life, forming a flock which will only be finally established when time ends. Through the sacraments, understood in their complete meaning of revelation and life, Christ, who entrusted them to the hierarchy of His Church, is constantly in action on earth. He remains present in order to realize His heart's desire; He is present through the communication of His priesthood, through the grace He gives, through the glory He promises, through the Holy Spirit who is both the Gift to believers and the agent that unites mankind: "The imparting of the Holy Spirit be with you all" (2 Cor 13:13). "That they all be one . . . so as to see my glory" (Jn 17:21, 24).

Lastly, when we live from the sacraments, we are preparing on earth the Church of heaven. "The man who eats this bread will live eternally" (Jn 6:59). The ultimate purpose of the sacraments is eternal life; that is why they foretell the future glory of the heavenly Jerusalem and begin its construction among men. . . .

They begin its construction since they pour into each of us living water, not only for this world but for everlasting life (Jn 4:14); water for the thirsty man, for the man of desires, the drink which God and the Lamb will bestow on the wedding day of the Bridegroom and the Bride (Rev 22:17). "In that place you will show me all that my heart desired" (St. John of the Cross, *Spiritual Canticle*, v. 36). This desire, St. John of the Cross explains, is the perfect union with God in love, a union that cannot be completed in this life. . . .

The sacraments also prepare us for the life and activities of the heavenly Jerusalem by the zest they give us in our search for God. On earth, their psychological function is wholly ordained to the discovery of God's nature, to His mystery as manifested in Christ, to the total development of man's potentialities. In the heavenly city all this will have disappeared and God will be "all in all." But the common and fraternal love of God, then unrestrictedly present, will continue. Praise will be unending in eternal rest; love will be for ever new and will for ever increase. "There we shall rest and we shall see; we shall see and we shall love; we shall love and we shall praise" (St. Augustine, *City of God*, 22, 30).

— "What Is a Sacrament," in *The Twentieth Century Encyclopedia of Catholicism*, 172–174

⚬ Quiet Time and Then Discussion ⚬

Questions for Meditation

1. Should I think some more about the sacraments and how I assist at them?

2. Can I do something additional to assist properly at the sacraments?

3. If I know non-Catholic Christians who are receiving valid sacraments like Baptism and Matrimony, do I take the opportunity to tell them what this all means?

Prayer

O Lord Jesus Christ, how much You have loved us! You have given us these mysterious signs of Your living grace. By Your Holy Spirit give me the faith to assist at or to receive the sacraments as best I can. Help me always to give a good example of reverence and faith at Your sacraments. Amen.

The Sacrament of Baptism

READINGS
Acts 16:31–33; Romans 6:3–4;
Catechism *1213–1233*

Baptism is the first of the three Sacraments of Initiation, and Confirmation and Holy Eucharist are the other two. They are called this because this trio of sacraments provides the foundation of the Christian life. Through Baptism we are freed from sin — both original sin and sins we have actually committed — and we are born again as God's adopted children. Baptism opens up for us the life of grace; it makes us members of the Church, the Mystical Body of Christ, and it gives us access to all the other sacraments. The words of St. Gregory of Nazianzus, cited in paragraph 1216 of the *Catechism*, sum up the effects of Baptism very beautifully:

> Baptism is God's most beautiful and magnificent gift....
> We call it gift, grace, anointing, enlightenment, garment

of immortality, bath of rebirth, seal, and most precious gift. It is called gift because it is conferred on those who bring nothing of their own; grace, since it is given even to the guilty; Baptism, because sin is buried in the water; anointing, for it is priestly and royal as are those who are anointed; enlightenment, because it radiates light; clothing, since it veils our shame; bath, because it washes; and seal, as it is our guard and the sign of God's Lordship.

Baptism should be given ordinarily in the parish church by a priest or deacon. In case of necessity, however, as when an infant is in danger of death, Baptism can be given anywhere by anyone who intends to do what Jesus commanded. Following its ancient tradition for adults, the Church has reestablished several steps leading to Baptism; they are called the Rite of Christian Initiation of Adults (RCIA). The person to be baptized must be in the catechumenate for a period of several months before Baptism is conferred. The Baptism of children does not require this, but pastoral instruction is often provided, usually by the parish. When the sacrament of Baptism is conferred on an adult, the Church presumes that person to be seriously converted and means to follow Christ's teaching and continue to grow in faith.

It can be spiritually very fruitful to think of our own Baptism, even if we received this sacrament as infants. When I perform Baptisms, I remind everyone that what we are doing will last forever. A spiritual seal, often called a character, marks a person's soul. These are, of course, mysterious things. That sign, or seal, will accompany the baptized person forever, whether in heaven or hell. The grace of Baptism cannot work if it is blocked by deliberate serious sin. I have observed that a baptized person who has given up the practice of the faith is never comfortable again and may surprise us by a second conversion. We who have been baptized into Christ and cleansed by His Precious Blood should value Baptism immeasurably, and we should try to see that others take their Baptism seriously.

Quotation for Meditation

I speak to you who have just been reborn in Baptism, my little children in Christ, you who are the new offspring of the Church, gift of the Father, proof of Mother Church's fruitfulness. All of you who stand fast in the Lord are a holy seed, a new colony of bees, the very flower of our ministry and fruit of our toil, my joy and my crown. It is the words of the Apostle that I address to you: "Put on the Lord Jesus Christ, and make no provision for the flesh and its desires," so that you may be clothed with the life of him whom you have put on in this sacrament. "You have all been clothed with Christ by your baptism in him. There is neither Jew nor Greek; there is neither slave nor freeman; there is neither male nor female; you are all one in Christ Jesus."

Such is the power of this sacrament: it is a sacrament of new life which begins here and now with the forgiveness of all past sins, and will be brought to completion in the resurrection of the dead. "You have been buried with Christ by baptism into death in order that, as Christ has risen from the dead, you also may walk in newness of life."

You are walking now by faith, still on pilgrimage in a mortal body away from the Lord; but he to whom your steps are directed is himself the sure and certain way for you: Jesus Christ, who for our sake became man. For all who fear him he has stored up abundant happiness, which he will reveal to those who hope in him, bringing it to completion when we have attained the reality which even now we possess in hope.

— St. Augustine, Sermon 8, *Liturgy of the Hours*, II, 635

Გᴸᴼ Quiet Time and Then Discussion Გᴸᴼ

Questions for Meditation

1. Do I think prayerfully of my Baptism sometimes?
2. Do I know the exact date and place of my Baptism, and the priest's name who baptized me?

3. Do I show concern for the new evangelization so that others may be called to the grace of Baptism?

Prayer

O Lord Jesus, how grateful I am for the grace of Baptism and for the Baptism of so many who are dear to me. Eternal life — that is what I have received. Send this grace of the Holy Spirit on us all. Permit that we may help others to receive this sacrament and that all may rise to eternal life with You. Amen.

Meditation Ten

The Rites of Baptism and Their Spiritual Meaning

❧

READINGS
Acts 2:38–41; Romans 6:3–11, 17; Galatians 3:27–28;
Catechism *1234–1244*

When we attend a Baptism, we are aware of several ceremonies surrounding the sacrament. Often, though, we pay little attention to them, focusing only on the actual Baptism: the pouring of the water and the Trinitarian formula or invocation of the Holy Trinity. Actually, the other ceremonies have important spiritual significance to which we should pay careful attention, especially when we meditate on the graces we have received either as infants or adults in our own Baptisms. The *Catechism* refers to this as the mystagogy of the celebration (CCC 1234).

The Sign of the Cross begins the rite. Here the celebrant and others make the sign of the cross on the forehead of the person to be baptized. In this we are claimed for Christ at our Baptisms by the very sign of the Redemption.

Readings from sacred Scripture, especially the Gospel, follow, reminding us that Baptism is a sacrament of faith. We must accept faith and practice it. Love for the Bible and especially for the Gospel is one sign of a true Christian.

The Deliverance from Evil, or the exorcism, often goes unnoticed, except that we are called on to reject Satan and evil in all its forms. In these days when there are so many evil influences around us, particularly in the media, when chaos seems a characteristic of nearly every aspect of daily life, the exorcism should take on new and important meaning, especially in adult Baptism. The anointing with the oil of catechumens is a sign of divine protection, one we should take seriously. This custom derives from the ancient practice of soldiers who, when going into battle, anointed their bodies so that weapons or other objects hurled at them might slip off without doing any harm.

The Blessing of the Baptismal Water calls to our minds the many uses of water in salvation history, and these are recounted in a beautiful prayer recited at Baptisms. Little known is the fact that water taken from the River Jordan for Baptism does not require a blessing; it has been eternally blessed by the Baptism of Christ.

THE RITES OF BAPTISM AND
THEIR SPIRITUAL MEANING

The actual Baptism, which means to submerge, signifies the act of burying someone. As burial happens after death, this burial in water indicates a death to sin in the life of the one who has been buried. The reemergence from the water, of course, is a rising to new life — life in Christ. Water and immersion in it have been used as symbols of death and new life by many traditional religions. Understanding this, St. Paul powerfully stresses the image of death and resurrection with Christ as the explanation of the symbolism of Baptism.

The Anointing with Holy Chrism comes next. In it the person who receives the sacrament of Baptism is anointed with oil consecrated in Holy Week by the bishop. This is a special mixture perfumed with balm and is used in the rites for three sacraments: Baptism, Confirmation, and Holy Orders (the ordination of priests and bishops). In earlier times it was used also to anoint kings and queens at their coronations. The use of Holy Chrism indicates that all who are baptized are part of a priestly people, a royal people preparing for the kingdom of God.

The white garment symbolizes the putting on of Christ of which we read in St. Paul's letter to the Galatians (Gal 3:27), and the white candle reminds us of the immortality of the soul and that we who are baptized into Christ are to be a light to the world.

All the symbols and customs that surround the sacrament of Baptism have great meaning and profound depth. When we attend a Baptism, it is helpful to appreciate all these symbols and try prayerfully to apply them to our Christian life.

Quotation for Meditation

And this is the meaning of the great sacrament of Baptism which is solemnized among us, that all who attain to this grace should die to sin, as He is said to have died to sin, because He died in the flesh, which is the likeness of sin; and rising from the font regenerate, as He arose alive from the grave, should begin a new life in the Spirit, whatever may be the age of the body.

For from the infant newly born to the old man bent with age, as there is none shut out from Baptism, so there is none who in Baptism does not die to sin. But infants die only to original sin; those who are older die also to all the sins which their evil lives have added to the sin which they brought with them....

[O]ne sin, admitted into a place where such perfect happiness reigned, was of so heinous a character, that in one man the whole human race was originally, and as one may say, radically, condemned; and it cannot be pardoned and blotted out except through the one Mediator between God and men, the man Christ Jesus, who only has had power to be so born as not to need a second birth....

All the events, then, of Christ's crucifixion, of His burial, of His resurrection the third day, of His ascension into heaven, of His sitting down at the right hand of the Father, were so ordered that the life which the Christian leads here might be modeled upon them, not merely in a mystical sense but in reality. For in reference to His crucifixion it is said: "They that are Christ's have crucified the flesh, with the affections and lusts." And in reference to His burial: "We are buried with Him by Baptism into death." In reference to His resurrection: "That, as Christ was raised up from the dead by the glory of the Father, even so we also should walk in newness of life." And in reference to His ascension into heaven and sitting down at the right hand of the Father: "If ye then be risen with Christ, seek those things which are above, where Christ sitteth on the right hand of God. Set your affection on things above, not on things on the earth. For ye are dead, and your life is hid with Christ in God."

— St. Augustine, *Enchiridion*,
Chapters 42 [pp. 52–53], 43 [p. 53],
48 [p. 58], 53 [pp. 63–64]

☙ Quiet Time and Then Discussion ❧

Questions for Meditation

1. Do I think of my Baptism occasionally and what it means to me?

2. Do I consider that my Baptism calls me to avoid sin; that if I sin, I am called to repentance and reconciliation?

3. Do I ever take the trouble to remind others of their Baptism and its meaning?

Prayer

Lord Jesus, I was baptized into Your death and washed clean by Your blood. Help me grow each day in the grace of Baptism. Help me also to avoid sin and to "put on Christ." You paid so much for my redemption. Help me make a return for Your love, a return that opens my being to grow in Your grace. Amen.

Meditation Eleven

Who Can Be Baptized?

READINGS
Mark 16:15–16; John 3:5; 1 Corinthians 12:12–13;
Catechism *1246–1256*

Baptism implies a commitment to Christ as one's Savior as well as a promise to follow His teaching. It also implies a belief in and acceptance of the entirety of the Christian faith. Each person who wishes to be baptized, therefore, must seriously promise to fulfill the dictates of faith and love. Of course, it is understood that no one is able to live the life of faith perfectly. We are limited by sin and cannot hope to attain the lofty goals of the Christian life in their totality. But this fact does not excuse us. We commit ourselves to obey the laws of Christ and the Gospel as best we can. If sins are to be forgiven, they must be repented of. This is why the rite of Baptism contains a rejection of evil and a profession of faith. The rite of adult Baptism involves a long preparation, a catechesis that progresses slowly through various stages, making this need for conversion more obvious. We learn much in our meditations when we go over the things to which we are committed by Baptism.

We also learn something important from the Baptism of children, the retarded, and the mentally ill. Such Baptisms are not recognized by the denominations that require confessional Baptism — what we Catholics call the Baptism of adults, with all the responsibilities listed above. It is the belief of these denominations that Baptism requires a firm profession of faith in all cases and therefore can be received only by adults of sound mind. This has never been the Church's understanding. Before the end of the persecutions in the early Church there are descriptions of the Baptism of infants and of children too young to make a commitment to Christ themselves. In those days as in these, the children's parents or guardians spoke for them. The important truth here is that God does not make Baptism depend absolutely on the profession of faith for those who cannot make one. The Church does require one, however, in the case of an adult or older child capable of consent and commitment. Our salvation is the work of Christ, and we show our loyalty in following His teaching through good works. Such a profession of faith is a very good work, although most of us don't think of it in those terms. It is a paradox that the very denominations who claim to deny the need for good works require this one for Baptism. Of course a person capable of a commitment to Christ must make one, but salvation is essentially Christ's work. We should not attempt to limit Him. These same denominations also require that the minister of Baptism be a committed evangelical Christian. Again, this is not the Church's position. In the early Church in the case of extreme necessity (for example, in the case of a catechumen about to be martyred), even an unbaptized person could be requested to baptize if he or she intended to do what Christ had commanded. The minister at Baptism simply stands in for Jesus. It is Christ who baptizes; it is He who saves. And He saves us by incorporating us into His divine life. This is the source of all hope for eternal life.

Quotation for Meditation

"If anyone denies that infants newly born from their mothers' wombs are to be baptized," even though they be born of baptized parents, "or says they are baptized indeed for the remission of sins, but that they derive nothing of original sin from Adam, which must be expiated by the laver of regeneration" for the attainment of life everlasting, whence it follows, that in them the form of Baptism for the remission of sins is understood to be not true, but false: let him be anathema. For what the Apostle has said: "By one man sin entered into the world, and by sin death, and so death passed upon all men, in whom all have sinned (Rom

5:12), is not to be understood otherwise than as the Catholic Church spread everywhere has always understood it.

For by reason of this rule of faith from a tradition of the Apostles even infants, who could not as yet commit any sins of themselves, are for this reason truly baptized for the remission of sins, so that in them there may be washed away by regeneration, what they have contracted by generation. "For unless a man be born again of water and the Holy Ghost, he cannot enter into the kingdom of God" (Jn 3:5).

— From the Council of Trent (1546)

⁓ Quiet Time and Then Discussion ⁓

Questions for Meditation

1. Do I understand why the Church has always called for the Baptism of children and of people who are mentally retarded?
2. Have I thought about the fact that Christ is the real person who baptizes?
3. Do I think of my commitments as one of the baptized?

Prayer

O Lord Jesus Christ, how grateful we must be to know that we are washed in the waters of Baptism, really the waters sanctified by Your precious Blood. Help us each day, each hour, to be faithful to You and to recognize You always as Lord and Master, our brother, and our hope for eternal life. And let the saving bath of Your divine charity wash over all I know and over the whole human race. Amen.

Meditation Twelve

The Effects of Baptism

READINGS
Romans 8:12–17; Galatians 3:26–29; 1 Peter 1:3–11;
Catechism *1262–1270*

When we consider that Baptism is one of the most important things that can happen to us, it is surprising that we think so little of its effects. Through Baptism we have the possibility of eternal life, which is really a divine prerogative. Eternal life is not an essential component of human nature, and it is very far from being a human right. It is an absolute gift of God, an almost unfathomable promise. In Baptism we are given the forgiveness of sins from the past and the promise of forgiveness in the future if we repent. The terrible effect of original sin — the loss of the possibility of eternal life — is removed. In a real sense we become new creatures, ones in whose inmost being dwells the Holy Trinity. We are able to believe in God, hope in Him, and even love Him with a love beyond our own self-concern. Baptism enables us to perform virtuous actions in union with Christ — acts which then contribute to our salvation. Christ operates in us. He is the vine; we are the branches.

Because of these spiritual realities, we can be said to be part of the Mystical Body of Christ. This is a deeply mysterious concept. There is nothing in our human experience that resembles it, to which we can compare it. Christ lives in us and we in Him. Our good deeds become His good deeds. We pray that His mind will be in us (see Phil 2:5).

Original sin is removed at Baptism, but its lasting effects are not. Therefore, the life of the Christian is one of endless struggle. Knowing this, Our Lord admonishes us to carry our cross, and St. Paul encourages us to fight the good fight (1 Tim 6:12). What are we fighting if we have "become a new creation in Christ"? St. Augustine gives us an insight here. He teaches that the effects of original sin that remain become the battleground of the spiritual life. They are:

1. The darkening of the intellect
2. The weakening of the will
3. Emotional confusion
4. Discord among human relationships, especially close ones

The seven capital sins — pride, covetousness, lust, anger, envy, gluttony, and sloth — are part of the drama of the spiritual battle. Baptism prepares us for the battle, and Confirmation, which in the early Church was given with Baptism, strengthens us for the battle, which continues until we close our eyes on this world and render an account to our blessed Savior in the world to come.

Quotation for Meditation

Baptism, with faith in Jesus Christ, has become for us the sacrament of divine adoption and Christian initiation. It is in the name of the Holy Trinity that it is conferred upon us, the Trinity that was revealed to us on the banks of the Jordan.

Sanctified by contact with the humanity of Jesus, and united to the "Word of truth," the water has the virtue of washing away the sins of those who detest their faults and declare their faith in the divinity of Christ; it is the Baptism not only of water "for the remission of sins," but of the Spirit who alone can "renew the face of the earth." From being "children of wrath" as we were, it makes us children of God, so that we are henceforward with Jesus, although in a lesser measure, the objects of the heavenly Father's delight.

St. Paul says that we have by Baptism put off the old man (descended from Adam) with the works of death, and have put on the new man created in justice and truth (the soul regenerated by the Word and the Holy Spirit) who is renewed unceasingly "according to the image of Him that created him."

In the same way that Baptism constituted for Christ the summary of His mission, at once redeeming and sanctifying, so Baptism contains for us in germ the whole development of the Christian life with its twofold aspect of "death to sin" and of "life unto God."

So true is it, according to the Apostle's words, that "as many . . . as have been baptized in Christ, have put on Christ"; so true is it that we make only one with Jesus in all His mysteries.

O happy state of faithful Christians! O foolish blindness of those who forget their baptismal promises! O terrifying destiny of those who tread them underfoot!

— Blessed Columba Marmion, *Christ in His Mysteries*

∾ Quiet Time and Then Discussion ∾

Questions for Meditation

1. While in life's struggle, do I recall that I am committed to that struggle by Baptism?
2. Do I take advantage of my incorporation into Christ in order to overcome the evil effects of original sin?

3. Do I encourage other Christians, whether Catholic or not, in their struggle to lead truly Christian lives by fighting the good fight?

Prayer

O Lord Jesus Christ, You have made me a member of Your mystical body. My good deeds, done with grace, are Your good deeds. I strive to have Your mind in me. It is a long, difficult struggle, but You suffered and died on the Cross in order to have Your Precious Blood wash away the sins of the world — my sins. Help me, O Lord, to appreciate what You have done for me and by holy Baptism to begin to be a new creature according to Your will. Amen.

Meditation Thirteen

The Seal of the Holy Spirit

◈

READINGS
Luke 4:16–22; Matthew 3:13–17; John 1:33–34;
Catechism *1286–1292*

Sacraments are ultimately mysteries; comprehension of the true essence of a sacrament exceeds the limits of our human minds. Yet we are granted partial knowledge. We understand that through the sacraments God's grace is bestowed upon us, that the sacraments are essential to our spiritual lives, that in many mysterious ways they bring us to God and bring God to us. When we think of Baptism and Confirmation, we know them to be Sacraments of Initiation and so might be tempted to think of them solely in this sense, as entranceways into the Mystical Body of Christ. But in truth they are infinitely more. As stated in Meditation Twelve, "Baptism prepares us for battle, and Confirmation, which in the early church was given with Baptism, strengthens us for the battle." St. Paul writes of this same spiritual battle in his letter to the Romans: "I appeal to you therefore, brethren, by the mercies of God, to present your bodies as a living sacrifice, holy and acceptable to God, which is your spiritual worship. Do not be conformed to this world but be transformed by the renewal of your mind, that you may prove what is the will of God, what is good and acceptable and perfect" (Rom 12:1).

The sacrament of Confirmation completes baptismal grace. Confirmation makes available to the faithful the strength of the Holy Spirit and can be considered a personal Pentecost for each of us. When we are confirmed, the same graces the Apostles received after Christ's Ascension are given to us. In Confirmation we are strengthened and sealed by the Spirit. In Confirmation, as in all sacraments, we are transformed by the grace of God. The confirmed believer stands on a firm foundation and can proclaim with the faithful — past, present, and future — the words of St. Paul: "I can do all things in him who strengthens me" (Phil 4:13).

The graces we receive at Confirmation are an awesome gift and a profound responsibility. The Spirit enters our lives in a new way, empowering us to live for Christ, sending us out to evangelize for Him, enabling us to overcome our fallen nature and the temptations of a sin-darkened world. But we cannot leave it all up to the Holy Spirit. We must accept the transformation that God offers us in Confirmation. We must welcome the Holy Spirit into our lives, as did the Apostles on Pentecost. We must become true soldiers of Christ.

The very essence of the rite of Confirmation is the gift of the Spirit, whose seal marks the baptized as Christians. In the ancient world one's seal was like a modern person's signature. Impressed in wax on a document, it identified the author. Tattooed on the forearm of a Roman soldier, it identified him as belonging to a particular legion. Branded on animals, it became a mark of ownership. The outpouring of the Holy Spirit seals Christians with the sign of the cross and becomes the mark of their salvation. St. Paul referred to himself as a slave for Christ, signifying his total self-abandonment to the God who was revealed to him in Jesus Christ.

All that we accomplish in and through Christ can be attributed to the anointing and sealing of the Holy Spirit we received in Confirmation. We are reminded of this powerful truth every time we read the words of St. Paul in his letter to the Ephesians: "Now to him who by the power at work within us is able to do far more abundantly than all that we ask or think, to him be glory" (Eph 3:20).

Quotation for Meditation

In the believer, the Holy Spirit develops the entire dynamism of the grace which gives new life and of the virtues which translate this vitality into fruits of goodness. From "within" the believer the

Holy Spirit is also at work like a fire, according to another simile, used by John the Baptist regarding baptism: "He will baptize you with the Holy Spirit and fire" (Mt 3:11). Jesus himself also used it regarding his messianic mission: "I have come to set the earth on fire" (Lk 12:49). The Spirit, therefore, stirs up a life with that fervor which St. Paul recommends in his letter to the Romans: "Be fervent in the Spirit" (Rom 12:11). This is the "living flame of love" which purifies, enlightens, burns, and consumes, as St. John of the Cross has explained so well.

Under the action of the Holy Spirit in the believer an original sanctity is developed that it assumes, elevates, and brings the personality of each one to perfection without destroying it. Thus, every saint has his own physiognomy. As St. Paul can say: "Star differs from star in glory" (1 Cor 15:41), not only in a "future resurrection" to which Paul refers but also in the present condition of the person who is no longer merely psychic (endowed with natural life) but spiritual (enlivened by the Holy Spirit) (cf. 1 Cor 15:44 ff).

— Pope John Paul II, *The Spirit, Giver of Life and Love*, 386

◈ Quiet Time and Then Discussion ◈

Questions for Meditation

1. How has Confirmation strengthened you as one of the faithful?

2. What is St. Paul asking the believer to surrender to God, and have I succeeded in doing this?
3. How does Confirmation help me to continue in my personal renewal, and how does it help me to evangelize others?

Prayer

Father of Light, from whom every good gift comes,
send your Spirit into our lives
with the power of a mighty wind,
and by the flame of your wisdom
open the horizons of our minds.
Loosen our tongues to sing your praise
in word beyond the power of speech.
For without your Spirit
man could never raise his voice in words of peace
or announce the truth that Jesus is Lord,
who lives and reigns with you and the Holy Spirit,
one God forever and ever. Amen.

— Alternative opening prayer for Mass
During the Day on Pentecost

Meditation Fourteen

Anointing with the Oil of Gladness

~

READINGS
1 Samuel 16:1–13; Acts 8:15–17; Acts 10:38;
Catechism *1293–1301*

According to the *Catechism of the Catholic Church*, the sign of the spiritual seal of the Holy Spirit which we receive at Confirmation is an anointing with oil. This post-baptismal anointing with sacred Chrism signifies a consecration. It marks an individual as having been set apart for a specific calling. The Christian who has received the sacrament of Confirmation is one who has been set apart for God to work in and through.

To the Hebrews, anointing was often a sign of royalty. The Kings of Israel were not crowned but were anointed with oil. The word "Messiah" in Hebrew means the anointed one. When we translate from Hebrew into Greek, "Messiah" is rendered "Christ," a word derived from "Chrism," a Greek word for oil.

From this we readily understand that when we proclaim Jesus to be the Christ, we proclaim Him to be the Anointed One of God, the Messiah, the true King of Israel, and the King of Kings.

The Hebrew Scriptures also show us that anointing could be a sign of profound hospitality. By anointing an important visitor, one welcomed this guest into one's home and made him aware that all one's possessions were his. In this context, anointing indicated an unconditional welcome.

In the anointing we receive at Confirmation, we find both traditions of our Hebrew ancestors in faith to be alive. When Jesus was baptized by John, the Holy Spirit descended upon Him in a spiritual anointing, showing Him to be the long-hoped-for Messiah. But as the *Catechism* teaches us: "This fullness of the Spirit was not to remain uniquely the Messiah's but was to be communicated to the whole messianic people" (CCC 1287). When we are anointed at Confirmation, we receive the same spirit who descended on Jesus in the Jordan; we are given a royal role as part of the messianic people; we are welcomed fully into the Body of Christ.

The Church views the anointing of Confirmation with a profound sense of importance. This is shown clearly in the way the chrism used at Confirmation is consecrated. The *Catechism* tells us, "It is the bishop who in the course of the Chrism Mass of Holy Thursday consecrates the sacred chrism for his whole diocese" (CCC 1297). When we consider this, we are reminded of the letter to the Hebrews, which states: ". . . thy God has anointed thee with the oil of gladness beyond thy comrades" (Heb 1:9b).

We must live the sacrament of Confirmation continuously. We must remember that God has welcomed us without reservation and anointed us a royal people with royal responsibilities. Let us pray that the anointing we received at Confirmation will give us the strength to allow God to work in and through us every day of our lives.

Quotation for Meditation

The Holy Spirit's teaching is unction. He teaches us by pouring himself into us gently and penetratingly. His teaching is as a divine caress of love. He teaches us as mothers teach their children, with kisses of love, with an indefinable outpouring of tenderness. We learn from him as we perceive the fragrance of a perfume, as we savor the sweetness of a fruit or enjoy the caress of a breeze that enfolds us.

The light of the Holy Spirit is the fruit of love; it is the happy consequence of union. United intimately to divine things through the work of the Holy Spirit, the soul tastes them by a direct divine experience. How profoundly do the words of St. John express this: "His anointing teaches you concerning all things."

But light is not the only mark of the direction of the Spirit; there is also sanctity. As the artist is not content with explaining to his pupil the secrets of art, but takes the uncertain hand of the beginner, and gently but firmly moves and guides it in order that the beauty of his ideal may be expressed on the canvas, even thus does the Holy Spirit take our faculties and move and guide them, so firmly that they do not stray, and at the same time so gently that our activities continue to be vital, spontaneous, and free. Only the creator can reach in this way to the depths of our acts and, so far from changing their properties, rather marvelously perfect and elevate them.

— Archbishop Luis M. Martinez,
True Devotion to the Holy Spirit, 18-19

❧ Quiet Time and Then Discussion ☙

Questions for Meditation

1. What does the sacrament of Confirmation truly confirm in us?

2. What significance is drawn from the Old Testament regarding Confirmation?

3. How have you experienced the Holy Spirit in your own life? How did this change you?

Prayer

Come, Holy Spirit, Light of souls!
Open our eyes, that we may perceive the wonders in our
heart!
Enlighten us, move us, quicken us, prompt us,
that we may forget this poor exterior world, so deficient and
imperfect,
and may live in that other, interior world where Thou art
and where, like a splendid Sovereign,
Thou dost give us Thy gifts of infinite power.
Amen.

— Archbishop Luis M. Martinez,
True Devotion to the Holy Spirit, 151

Meditation Fifteen

The Gift of Confirmation

READINGS
Romans 8:11–27; Luke 24:45–53; Catechism *1302–1311*

As Fr. Benedict Groeschel so beautifully explains in his book *In the Presence of Our Lord*, "The sacraments are objective realities, really pledges given by Christ through His Church that the grace and mercy of God will flow upon us by a devout and believing fulfillment of the sacred sign. In recent decades theologians have emphasized the essential link between the seven sacraments and the Church herself, which can in a certain way be called the fundamental sacrament."

He also reminds us that, "The Latin word '*sacramentum*' simply means a pledge or promise to give something, an IOU given by God, not so different in this respect from the covenant promises given in the Old Testament to Israel. The Greek word most often used for a sacrament, '*mysterion*,' stresses the invisible power of the sacramental sign; this term finds its root in the Greek verb 'to close one's eyes.' It stresses the invisible effects of the

95

sacrament. Because they are external or perceptible promises of the immense reality of grace, of God's covenant of mercy with His children, sacraments are signs, but they are effective signs, not merely symbolic ones. They cause what they signify. God in His love binds Himself to His creatures."[6]

We must remember, therefore, that Confirmation is not simply a ritual developed by the Church, a kind of graduation ceremony, even one rich in meaning and history. It is rather, a mysterious supernatural reality instituted by God, one that truly marks our souls, changing us forever. The effects of the sacrament of Confirmation include a deepening of the baptismal graces. Some of these effects are that:

1. Our spirit now bears witness to our nature as children of God.
2. We become strengthened in our relationship with Jesus Christ.
3. The gifts of the Holy Spirit increase in our walk with Him.
4. Our bond with the Church becomes stronger.
5. The Holy Spirit enables us to spread the faith and boldly defend it as witnesses for Jesus Christ who are not ashamed of the Cross.

Such changes are profound and should not be taken lightly. They should be understood as enabling us to become ever more like Christ as we journey to the Father. When we reflect upon the earthly life of our Lord, we see that He was constantly and intimately connected to the Holy Spirit. It is an article of our faith that Jesus was conceived by the Holy Spirit; the same Spirit descended upon Him at His Baptism, and before His return to the Father Jesus promised to send us the Holy Spirit as the Counselor. In fulfillment of that promise, with power from on high, the Spirit descended upon the Apostles on the Feast of Pentecost, enabling them to go forth in courage and in faith to spread the Good News of Jesus Christ. In Confirmation we, too, become intimately connected to the Holy Spirit, connected to God himself.

In the sacrament of Confirmation, we are given the same graces that the Apostles received on Pentecost, and with those graces come an increased responsibility to act as mature Christians — to live every moment of our lives as followers of Christ, as imitators of Christ. No baptized Catholic should go through life without the sacrament of Confirmation. The unconfirmed should waste no time in seeking out an RCIA program that will lead them to the reception of this sacrament. As confirmed Catholic Christians, it is not enough for us to know our faith in a superficial way. We must constantly learn about it and be growing in it. Solid teaching (catechesis) is essential if we are to gain a full appreciation of the Spirit's wonderful gifts to us.

Quotation for Meditation

The Holy Spirit brings about our sanctification in two ways. The first is by helping us, moving us, and directing us, but in such a way that we are actually doing our own work. It is our glory to fulfill our own destiny. God has given us the wonderful and terrible gift of freedom, by which we ourselves are the artisans of our own happiness or our own ruin.

But the Holy Spirit has another way of directing. It is His personal direction of our deeds, when He no longer merely illuminates us with His light, or warms us with his fire to show us the road that we must follow. In this second way, He Himself deigns to move our faculties and to urge us so that we may perform His work.

— Archbishop Luis M. Martinez,
True Devotion to the Holy Spirit, 128–129

❧ Quiet Time and Then Discussion ❧

Questions for Meditation

1. What is your level of commitment as a Catholic Christian in witnessing to others?
2. Were you ever a sponsor for a Confirmation candidate? If you stated yes, how did you fulfill your promises to encour-

age the candidate to live up to his or her commitment as a Catholic Christian?

3. What are some of the deepening effects of Confirmation in your life?

Prayer

Enter my heart, O Holy Spirit,
come in blessed mercy and set me free.
Throw open, O Lord, the locked doors of my mind;
cleanse the chambers of my thought for your dwelling:
light there the fires of thine own holy brightness in new
     understandings of truth,
O Holy Spirit, very God, whose presence is liberty,
grant me the perfect freedom
to be thy servant
today, tomorrow, evermore.
Amen.

— Eric Milner-White, as cited in
The Oxford Book of Prayer, 504

Meditation Sixteen

What We Can Expect
of Confirmation

READINGS
Acts: 2:1–47, 8:14–17; Catechism *1312–1321*

During the rite of Confirmation, the minister of the sacrament in both the Eastern and Western Churches anoints the candidate. In so doing, he brings to fulfillment an age-old promise established in sacred Scripture which states, "And it shall come to pass afterward, that I will pour out my spirit upon all flesh; your sons and your daughters shall prophesy, your old men shall dream dreams and your young men shall see visions. Even upon the menservants and maidservants in those days, I will pour out my spirit" (Joel 2:28–29).

Confirmation, which fulfills the promise of which we read in the book of Joel, transcends all age groups and includes all peoples. If one seeks liberating individuality without prejudice, then one is truly in search of the graces conferred at Confirmation.

Our Lord is the one who liberates us from ourselves by the power of the Holy Spirit, releasing mankind from the slavery of sin and confirming us in our relationship with God and His Holy Church. The prophet Joel wrote during a time when the children of God had rebelled and Judah was being invaded by swarms of devouring locusts. The people's crops had been destroyed, bringing famine. Total devastation seemed inevitable. If ever there was a time of bleak despair, it was then. Yet Joel's prophecy does not end in hopelessness and loss but speaks of eventual joy and fullness. In the name of the God of Israel, he promises almost more than can be imagined.

Confirmation makes real Joel's promises to each of us. This sacrament seals the power of God in the human soul, restoring what the locusts have destroyed in our lives. As it does this, it instills faith for service to God regardless of our individual inadequacies. Understanding this, St. Paul wrote: "For consider your call brethren; not many of you were wise according to worldly standards, not many were powerful, not many were of noble birth; but God chose what is foolish in the world to shame the wise, God chose what is weak in the world to shame the strong. God chose what is low and despised in the world, even things that are not, to bring to nothing things that are, so that no human being might boast in the presence of God" (1 Cor 1:26–29).

These words of St. Paul and the power of the Holy Spirit are illustrated vividly in the Acts of the Apostles. On the day of Pentecost, Peter, the terrified Apostle who denied Our Lord three times, addresses the people of Jerusalem. He does so, however, as a new Peter, one who has experienced the Holy Spirit. His abject fear is gone, replaced by faith and courage. He is transformed. The trembling Apostle has become the immovable rock upon which Christ has begun to build His Church. Peter boldly stands before a multitude to announce the fulfillment of Joel's prophecy and proclaim Jesus as the crucified and resurrected Messiah, the hope of all.

The grace of the Holy Spirit descends upon us in Confirmation, linking each of us to that long-ago day of Pentecost. The same Spirit who empowered the Apostles empowers us now. Let us pray never to ignore this transforming grace that has been given us at Confirmation. Let us pray never to impede it in any way.

Quotation for Meditation

Like the traveler pitching his tent in the desert, the Holy Spirit takes possession of souls as their most sweet guest. But unlike the traveler, who folds his tent as morning breaks, the eternal guest stays on. The tent he pitches in the soil of our barrenness is something divine — a sketch, a reflection, of our heavenly home. In it dwells grace that divinizes the soul, divine charity, the supernatural image of the Spirit who pours Himself into our hearts, and all the virtues and gifts. These are the conditions of His indwelling, so that He may begin His work of sanctification, and direct us with the strong, gentle influence of love.

His ideal is to reproduce Jesus in us, and through Jesus and with Jesus, to take us to the bosom of the Trinity and glorify the Father with the supreme glorification of Jesus. Through the shadows of faith, we . . . try to get a glimpse of this divine work, to see how, under the influence of the Holy Spirit, souls are purified, illuminated, and enkindled until they are transformed into Jesus, who is the ultimate ideal of God's love and of the aspirations of the soul, the glorious summit of the mystical ascent where we find peace and happiness — where we find God.

— Archbishop Luis M. Martinez,
True Devotion to the Holy Spirit, 49–50

❧ Quiet Time and Then Discussion ❧

Questions for Meditation

1. What type of people did the prophet Joel describe as recipients of the Holy Spirit? Why?

2. What can we expect from the Holy Spirit in the sacrament of Confirmation?

3. Why does one need to receive the sacrament of Confirmation?

Prayer

Come O Holy Spirit, Thou,
from the heavenly regions now.
Beams of light impart
on thy faithful who implore
and confess thee evermore.
In thy sevenfold gifts descend.
Give us virtue's sure reward.
Give us thy salvation, Lord.
Give us joys that never end. Amen.

Christ's Paschal Mystery Made Present

READINGS
Exodus 12, entire chapter; Luke 22:1–20 and 15:7;
Catechism *1322–1328*

On the day before he was given over to suffering and death, Our Lord ate the Passover dinner with His disciples. As the meal drew to a close He took unleavened bread and wine into His sacred hands and, blessing them, established the Eucharist. How mysterious and unfathomable this must have been to the Apostles as they received from the hands of our Divine Savior a bit of bread which He called His Body and a sip from a cup which He claimed contained not wine but His own Blood.

Christ was not bound to bring the Eucharist into being in this fashion. The God whose very thought is deed could have established His enduring mystical presence among us in an infinite variety of ways; yet He chose as the context for the Eucharist the Passover (or Paschal) dinner, a tradition already steeped in centuries of holiness. He chose to make the great thanksgiving that His followers would offer for His redemptive sacrifice (for "thanksgiving" is what *Eucharist* means in Greek) a meal that was already a solemn thanksgiving for God's acts of deliverance. A sacred obligation for all Jews from the time of the Exodus to the present, the Passover meal commemorates God's liberation of the Hebrew people from brutal Egyptian slavery. At Passover God freed His people from bondage, and as a free people they later accepted His covenant at Mount Sinai. God thus formed them into His chosen people to proclaim His sovereignty, live by His law, and one day give birth to His Messiah, His Christ.

As God's liberation of the Jewish people approached, the Paschal lamb was slain. Its blood was affixed to the doors of each Jewish household in Egypt, marking those homes as ones not to be visited by the angel of death who would force Pharaoh to free God's people. The lamb's flesh was then eaten during a meal of thanksgiving, which was the people's final act before passing over from the house of bondage into a new life of freedom.

In transforming the Passover meal into the first Eucharist, Jesus connects the long ago divine deliverance of the Jewish people to His own acts of redemption. He brings to fulfillment the promises implicit in the original Paschal event and reveals God's plan for the salvation of mankind. Taking upon Himself the role of the Paschal lamb, the victim whose blood is shed to bring on deliverance, He sacrifices himself for a world that is hopelessly mired in sin, whose relationship to God has been terribly wounded. As Jesus passes over from our corrupt and dying world to His heavenly Father, He liberates us from slavery to sin and death. He transforms us by His sacrifice, bringing us into a new relationship with God, a "new and everlasting covenant," one sealed in His own blood. Jesus, our Paschal victim, bridges the infinite distance between God and the sinful human soul, restoring the relationship to the divine that mankind had forfeited through sin, restoring it visibly in the Eucharist, the Paschal sacrament of His Body and Blood, the most intimate relationship possible between God and humanity, the most perfect sign of covenant imaginable.

When we kneel at Mass and watch the priest consecrate bread and wine just as Christ did on that Passover night, we should be in awe of the love which Christ shows for us in His Passover, in His Eucharist. We should have a fierce yearning to live the covenant that Christ's death and resurrection brought into being and abandon ourselves to the relationship to God that is made possible in the Eucharist. With St. Paul, we should joyfully proclaim: "Christ, our Passover, has been sacrificed for us; therefore let us keep the feast" (1 Cor 5:7–8).

Quotations for Meditation

If we wish to understand the power of Christ's Blood, we should go back to the ancient account of its prefiguration in Egypt. Sacrifice a lamb without blemish, commanded Moses, and sprinkle its blood on your doors. If we were to ask him what he meant, and how the blood of an irrational beast could possibly save men endowed with reason, his answer would be that the saving power lies not in the blood itself, but in the fact that it is a sign of the Lord's blood. In those days, when the destroying angel saw the blood on the doors, he did not dare to enter, so much less will the devil approach now when he sees not that figurative blood on the doors, but the true blood on the lips of believers, the doors of the temple of Christ.

— St. John Chrysostom, as cited in
Christian Prayer: The Liturgy of the Hours, 1985

———

Your chief aim in Holy Communion should be to advance, strengthen, and comfort yourself in the love of God; receiving for love's sake what love alone can give. There is nothing in which the love of Christ is set forth more tenderly or more touchingly than in the Sacrament, by which He, so to say, annihilates Himself for us, and takes upon him the form of bread, in order to feed us, and unite Himself closely to the bodies and souls of the faithful.

— St. Francis de Sales,
An Introduction to the Devout Life, 102

ᢒᢒ Quiet Time and Then Discussion ᢒᢒ

Questions for Meditation

1. The origins of the Christian Mass can be traced back to what important ritual meal?
2. Compare the Passover meal and the Last Supper. What important analogies can be made between the two?
3. What does the Eucharist, the Body, Blood, Soul, and Divinity of Christ mean to you?

Prayer

Lord Jesus Christ,
we worship You among us
in the sacrament of Your Body and Blood.
May we offer to our Father in heaven
a solemn pledge of undivided love.
May we offer to our brothers and sisters
a life poured out in loving service of that kingdom
where You live and reign with the Father and the Holy
*   Spirit,*
one God, for ever and ever. Amen.

— Alternative Opening Prayer for Corpus Christi

Meditation Eighteen

Sacrament of All Sacraments

READINGS
Colossians 1:24; 1 Corinthians 11:20; Revelation 19:9;
Matthew 14:19; 15–36; Mark 8:6, 19; Matthew 26:26;
1 Corinthians 11:24; Catechism *1329–1332*

The Holy Sacrifice of the Mass surpasses all sacrifices in the Old Covenant; it makes present the one sacrifice of Christ, of Our Lord and Savior.

Msgr. James O'Connor, author of *The Hidden Manna,* writes, "The realization that the Mass is the sacrifice of Christ and of the Church also helps toward an understanding of how each Mass is itself a sacrifice and not just an effective memorial of Calvary. To say that the Mass adds nothing to the sacrifice of the Cross is an imperfect understanding of how Christ effects our redemption. Jesus offered his sacrifice to the Father as a man and as mankind's priest and representative. That sacrifice was sufficient for the reconciliation of the entire world.

Nonetheless, Christ willed and wills to associate us with that sacrifice. St. Paul expresses this truth very strongly when he writes: 'Now I rejoice in what was suffered for you, and I fill up in my flesh what is still lacking in regard to Christ's afflictions, for the sake of his Body, which is the Church' (Col 1:24). By Christ's will, we bring more than Christ and His offering to the Father. As sacrificial offerings we also bring ourselves, and our own lives with their joys and sufferings. Taken up into the sacrifice of Christ, these too become part of the sacrifice of praise and propitiation presented to the Father. Thus, each Mass is a sacrifice in which something new is being offered, the constant accumulation of what the members of Christ offer with and in Him. In this way, in each sacrifice, the members of the body add their own merits to the merits of Christ. These merits are indeed totally dependent on Christ and come to us because of him and the work of his Spirit in us."[7]

When we refer to the Eucharist as the Most Blessed Sacrament, we acknowledge it as the sacrament of all sacraments. From the very beginning, the Church has always proclaimed the Eucharist to be nothing less than the true Body, Blood, Soul, and Divinity of Christ. His disciples recognized our Lord after the resurrection in the Breaking of the Bread. In Holy Communion we experience the risen Christ in an explicit way; in receiving His

Body and His Blood, we become united with Him and form one single body.

"In view of its overwhelming depth and breadth the mystery that Holy Communion is nothing less than a communion with the risen Christ Himself, a communion in which the recipient partakes of his Divine Master's very Body and Blood, it should not come as a surprise that the practice of adoring this sacrament outside the immediate context of the Eucharistic liturgy would take time to appear; the riches of God's gift of the Eucharist are too vast to be fully plumbed in the span of one generation. Yet the doctrines and observances from which extra-liturgical adoration is derived have been part of the deposit of faith since the apostolic era. The Church has always believed that the Eucharistic Presence of the Redeemer begins not at the moment of Communion but rather earlier, at the altar, brought about by the words and actions of Christ repeated by His ordained ministers. Coupled to this has been the belief that those unable to be present during the Mass itself were not to be deprived of receiving this sacrament, but rather that Christ remained present in the consecrated Eucharist Species even after the conclusion of the liturgy, making it possible to bring the sacrament to those who were ill or in prison. The testimony from the early centuries of the Church in regard to both these points is incontestable."[8]

Quotation for Meditation

St. Augustine saw the Eucharist as the binding element of the Church, the cement, as it were, that holds the faithful together, or, to use his own words, it is the chain of love (*vinculum caritatis*). He also emphasizes the reality of the Eucharistic Presence of Christ because it makes the sacrifice of the Mass real, in which Christ is "immolated . . . every day." He also presented the effects of the sacrament as very real, as it were, with a mystical realism: "Not only do we become Christians; we become Christ."

— Fr. Benedict J. Groeschel, C.F.R.,
In the Presence of Our Lord, 44

Quiet Time and Then Discussion

Questions for Meditation

1. If the sacrifice and atonement of Christ takes away all the sins of this world, why is it necessary for us to unite our suffering with His?

2. Why did the practice of adoring Christ's presence in the Eucharist develop in the Church?

3. In recent years there has been a decrease in devotion to the Eucharist. Has my personal devotion also decreased? What

do I really believe when I gaze upon the consecrated bread and wine and when I receive Holy Communion? In what ways can I increase my devotion?

Prayer

Lord God,
in return for thy great love
I would bring an offering.
But there is only one worthy offering:
The perfect obedience of thy Son
    even unto death.
Lord God,
    I remember that offering.
    I plead it before thee.
And though it be all-sufficient,
    I add to it
    the offering of myself,
    body, mind, and spirit,
    mind, heart, and will,
    all that I have,

all that I am,
all that by thy grace I can become.
Accept, O Lord God,
this unworthy sacrifice,
and cleanse
and sanctify
and use it
in the service of thy kingdom
for his dear sake.

— George Appleton, as cited in
The Oxford Book of Prayer, 534

The Holy Eucharist:
Sacrament of Unity

∿

READINGS
Psalm 104; John 14:8–17; John 16:12–15;
Catechism *1333–1344*

One of the prayers that may be said quietly by the priest shortly before he receives the Body and Blood of Christ at Mass contain these words: "Lord Jesus Christ, by the will of the Father and the work of the Holy Spirit, your death brought life to the world." A principle found enunciated in Holy Scripture and throughout the Church's history is reflected in this prayer: When Jesus along with the Father and the Holy Spirit are present, life is imparted. We take nothing from Jesus' uniqueness as the only Son of God when we say that He acts "through the will of the Father and the work of the Holy Spirit," for although we are fundamentally incapable of comprehending the mystery of the Triune God, we do know that the Father and the Spirit are always present in all that Jesus does and in all that He is. Jesus Himself articulates this in the Gospel of St. John with these words: "He who has seen me has seen the Father" (Jn 14:9).

Each person of the Trinity is unique, but together they are an indivisible unity — the unity of God. No person of the Trinity negates or contradicts another. How could they? They are, in essence, one. Trinity is fundamental to the nature of God, yet unity is as well. Nothing in the dogma of the Trinity contradicts the Shema, the famous Old Testament declaration of faith proclaimed by countless pious Jews — including Jesus Himself — over three millennia. "Hear, O Israel: the LORD our God is one LORD" (Deut 6:4) is a profession of faith that Christians can easily affirm without denying in any way the three persons that exist within the one God.

Psalm 104 is an exultant hymn to the God who made the universe. In rapt awe the psalmist catalogues one natural wonder after another, ascribing their being and their glory to the creative power of God. Like the psalmist, we stand in awe of the God whose will is the source of all things, but as Christians we do not lose sight of the fact that our Triune God reveals Himself to us not in creation alone but in redemption as well. The God who made heaven and earth is also the God who in Christ gives His life for the salvation of the world. The God who caused life to spring forth from inert matter also comes to us in the Eucharistic bread and wine, which are re-created into the Body and Blood of Christ.

As bread and wine are transformed in the Eucharist, so we are transformed when we receive the Eucharist. The Eucharist renews and makes present the Sacrifice of Calvary. It leads to God's ultimate saving act: the Resurrection. We see this in some of the most difficult and challenging words found in the Gospel of St. John, words that show clearly the place of the Eucharist in God's plan of redemption: ". . . unless you eat the flesh of the Son of man and drink his blood, you will have no life in you; he who eats my flesh and drinks my blood has eternal life and I will raise him up on the last day" (Jn 6:53, 54).

At every Mass, it is the Triune God, who makes the Eucharist possible, who offers us a new creation and a perfect redemption through what appear to be mere bread and wine. The Catholic at Mass should be in a state of exuberant celebration and awe because he knows that through the perfectly united will of the Father, the Son, and the Holy Spirit, we are offered the mystery of salvation and redemption once again.

Quotation for Meditation

St. Cyril, Archbishop of Jerusalem (c. 315–386), wrote: "The bread and wine of the Eucharist were simple bread before the invocation of the holy and adorable Trinity, but when the invocation has taken place the bread becomes the Body of Christ and the wine the Blood of Christ. . . .

The seeming bread is not bread even though it is sensible to the taste, but the body of Christ, and the seeming wine is not wine, even though the taste will have it so, but the Blood of Christ.

— *Catechetical Lectures* 19 and 20,
as cited by Aiden Nichols

Quiet Time and Then Discussion

Questions for Meditation

1. What principle do we see enunciated in the quotation found in the first paragraph of this meditation?
2. Trinity is fundamental to the nature of God. What other characteristic is as well?
3. In what way is salvation found and experienced in the Eucharist?

Prayer

O my Lord and God,
*   the journey is too great for me,*
*   unless*
*   thou feed me with the bread of heaven*
*   and wine of life,*
*   unless*
*   thou share with me thine own life*
*   victorious over sin,*
*   hatred, pain, and death.*
Let thy blood
*   flow through my veins*
*   thy strength be my strength*
*   thy love be my love*
*   And the father's will*
*   be my will as well as thine.*
Let me be one with thee
in heart, mind, and will.

— George Appleton, as cited in
The Oxford Book of Prayer, 535

The Holy Eucharist:
An Encounter with God

❦

READINGS
Leviticus 16, entire chapter; Hebrews 9:11–15; Luke 9:11–17;
Catechism *1345–1355*

It is vital to keep in mind the fundamental source of the Church's sacramental practices. These practices are not arbitrary in any way, but flow directly from Christ's Priestly offering. Holy Mass, of course, is the most vivid celebration of that offering. In joy and profound gratitude, we participate in the Eucharistic Liturgy, knowing that during it we receive the very Body and Blood of our Divine Savior. In the Eucharist, Christ's Priestly offering to the Father is made fully present. And in Holy Communion we become united with Christ — and through Him with the Father — in a way that is unequaled, a way too profound ever to be understood.

According to Mosaic Law, none of the Jewish people except the High Priest was permitted to enter the Holy of Holies, the inner sanctuary of the Temple. Even this was permissible only once each year, on Yom Kippur, the Day of Atonement. For the Jewish people, this sacred sanctuary deep within the recesses of the Temple was the special dwelling place of God, the one place on earth where the presence of Adonai was always assured, always palpable. Yet they believed they could never approach it. To them God was too exalted, too utterly transcendent to be fully encountered, even by the members of His Chosen People.

On Calvary, Jesus becomes both High Priest and sacrificial victim, and in so doing puts an end to the need for the sacrifices of the Temple. In His death and resurrection, our Savior reveals a startling truth to the world. He reveals that the utterly transcendent God worshiped by our Hebrew ancestors in faith is not simply the "God of power and might." He is not only the ineffable king who can never be directly encountered, whose very name is too holy to be uttered. He is a God whose love is so immeasurable that He will die for us, that He will feed us with His Body and Blood. In Christ, we learn that God yearns to be as palpably present in our souls as He was in the Holy of Holies in the Temple, that God wishes no distance to exist between Himself and those who love Him. The High Priest, as representative of the Jewish people, encountered the presence of God once each year on the Day of Atonement and brought God's blessing back to the people; so Christ, as our High Priest, turns Good Friday from a day of tragedy into a day of complete atonement and brings the presence of God to all who desire it.

Therefore, let us remember to receive the Eucharist with joy and reverence, with unfailing thankfulness to the God who allows us to encounter Him fully, who yearns to forgive our sins, to give us new life, and to turn our souls into His Holy of Holies.

Quotation for Meditation

We believe that the Word became flesh and that we receive his flesh in the Lord's Supper. How then can we fail to believe that he really dwells within us? When he became man, he actually clothed himself in our flesh, uniting it to himself forever. In the sacrament of his body he actually gives us his own flesh, which he has united with his divinity. This is why we are all one, because the Father is in Christ, and Christ is in us. He is in us through his flesh and we are in him. With him we form a unity which is in God.

— St. Hilary, as cited in
Christian Prayer: The Liturgy of the Hours, 2002

❧ Quiet Time and Then Discussion ❧

Questions for Meditation

1. What is the fundamental source of the Church's sacramental practices?

2. Why should our joy know no bounds when we receive the Eucharist?

3. What does Jesus teach us of the nature of God that was previously unknown?

Prayer

Nothing has been capable, dear Lord, to hinder you from being all mine; neither heaven, nor your divinity, nor the gibbet of the cross: grant me the grace that nothing may hinder me from being all yours, to whom I owe myself both for creation and redemption.

— Lady Lucy Herbert, as cited in
The Oxford Book of Prayer, 530

Meditation Twenty-One

The Holy Eucharist: The Path to Self-Giving and Contentment

◈

READINGS
An account of the Passion of Christ (Matthew 26–27; Mark 14–15; Luke 22–23; or John 18–20); Catechism 1356–1367

In the words of the great twentieth-century theologian Hans Urs von Balthasar, "The passivity of [Christ's] Passion, with its fetters, scourging, crucifixion, and piercing, is . . . the expression of a supremely active will to surrender and for that very reason transcends the limits of self-determination into the limitlessness of letting oneself be determined."[9]

What are we post-moderns to make of such strange words? A "supremely active will to surrender" is a blatant contradiction in terms to us. It is perplexing, disturbing. It is an affront. Active people never surrender. Passive ones do. And if there is one thing we claim to be sure of in our confused and confusing world, it is that constant activity is good. In activity we find our meaning. In activity we discover our worth. It is through activity that we triumph, that we achieve domination over others — an essential ingredient of life. But Christ, as always, teaches us new and deeper things about the meaning of human existence. In His Passion we are confronted with something we can't comprehend: a will that triumphs through surrender. And — as if that weren't disconcerting enough — we have a vague and troublesome suspicion that we're supposed to imitate this in some way.

A self-giving active will, however, would not have been an especially difficult concept to those who came before us, to the generations of Christians whose faith was profound, whose lives were lived in the great mystery of God's redemption of mankind. Such a will to them would simply have been one that had learned to be compliant with the movement of the Holy Spirit. For them, it was what we were all supposed to aspire to; it was that which would lead us to contentment.

Late in his life, St. Paul stated that he had learned to be content, implying that — even for a saint — arriving at this state involved a long process. If we are ever to come to the kind of contentment that Paul describes, we, too, will do it slowly, over long periods of time and in the midst of the fast-paced, sometimes chaotic activities of everyday life. This is a difficult journey, one beset by many obstacles. The world has always created barriers to true contentment, but the dramatically accelerated pace of present-day life can be so consuming that we forget that our lives have intrinsic value. We lose sight of the fact that what we do is distinct from what we are. Life is a pilgrimage that has as its destination eternity with God. It is this alone that gives meaning to our existence. For many people, including highly educated ones, however, all sense of life's purpose has faded into oblivion. Human existence is understood as little more than a series of appointments and errands jotted down in a daily planner, a never-ending catalogue of obligations to discharge. In the world's terms: we are what we do. To maintain our worth, to justify our very being, we must always be in the process of accomplishing something tangible. Life thus becomes drained of meaning and transformed into the senseless, endless task of Sisyphus who was condemned to push a heavy rock up a hill over and over again only to see it escape from his grasp at the last second and roll to the bottom again.

We must remember that the meaning of our lives transcends the material things we produce during them, that God has created us in His image, and that Jesus has given Himself on Calvary as our redeemer and continues to give Himself to us in the Eucharist until the end of time. The word "Eucharist" derives from a Greek word that means to be thankful, and in this word we find one of the keys to contentment. We must cultivate thankfulness to the God whose love knows no bounds. We must be mindful that we were created out of love and that at every instant our being is sustained out of love, that Christ gave His life for us out of love. The divine love does not depend on what we accomplish in this world or on how many possessions we accumulate, or what people think of us — it certainly doesn't depend on whom we can dominate. It depends on what we are: beings made for eternity with God. St. Paul — the most active of saints — came to this understanding. He encountered the divine love in a dramatic way on the road to Damascus and then met that same love over and over again in the Eucharist. In this meeting, he discovered a deeper meaning to life than any he had previously known. As we enter deeply and meditatively into the mystery of the Eucharist, we comprehend more and more the fact that Christ offers Himself to us in Holy Communion despite our limitations, our failures, and our constant relapses into sinfulness. Our imperfections cannot limit His love. If we remember this, we will live in a way that more clearly reveals our true nature. Perhaps we might even surrender our will a little, become compliant with the movement of the Holy Spirit, and achieve the contentment of which St. Paul speaks. Who knows, we might even learn to give of ourselves to others in some small imitation of Christ.

Quotation for Meditation

I bring to Mass today:

— my hopes and my needs, my trials and my fears;

— my gratitude for all that I have received from my Father's hand up to the present moment;

— my desire to remain close to my Father and come even closer to him during this day.

I come to the altar today:

— to give thanks for the daily mystery of my redemption and salvation;

— to seek the strength and perseverance that I find so lacking in myself;

— to seal again the covenant with God, my Father, in and through Jesus Christ my Lord.

— Terence Cardinal Cooke, *Prayers for Today*, 108

❧ Quiet Time and Then Discussion ❧

Questions for Meditation

1. Discuss the concept of a "self-giving active will." How is it possible for us to imitate Christ in this way?

2. In what do we find our true worth?

3. What are the elements of our lives that prevent us from see-ing ourselves as the beings that God created us to be?

Prayer

Anima Christi

Soul of Christ, sanctify me.
Body of Christ, save me.
Blood of Christ, inebriate me.
Water from the side of Christ, wash me.
Passion of Christ, strengthen me.
O good Jesus, hear me.
Within your wounds hide me.
Permit me never to be separated from you.
From the malicious enemy defend me.
At the hour of my death call me
and bid me come to you,
that, with your saints, I may praise you
forever and ever. Amen.

The Holy Eucharist: Pinnacle of Catholic Faith

READINGS
John 5:39–40; 6:35–40; Catechism 1368–1381

Prior to the Last Supper and His Crucifixion, the Lord demonstrated His divine nature by feeding the multitude with a few loaves and fish. His first public act was to change water into wine at the wedding feast of Cana. In compassion He healed the ill and the dying, including many who had lost all hope. He even transcended death by bringing Lazarus back from the grave.

It is impossible to believe in Christianity in its truest sense and not acknowledge God's infinite power over His creation, a power that we call miraculous. In demonstrating this power time and again, Jesus reveals Himself to be the second Person of the Blessed Trinity, the incarnate Son of God.

THE HOLY EUCHARIST:
PINNACLE OF CATHOLIC FAITH

Many non-Catholic Christians (and, sadly, in recent years some Catholics, as well) have professed a lack of belief in the Real Presence of Christ in the Eucharist. Yet often these same Christians are able to affirm that Jesus left His heavenly home to be born of the Virgin Mary as the only begotten Son of God. If one accepts the Incarnation, why then should one reject the Eucharist? If one believes in His coming as man, then why should one not be able to believe in His presence under the appearances of bread and wine? Could it be that we wish to limit the power of God to things our human minds can comprehend? Could it be that we do not truly believe the greatness of what our Father in heaven has prepared for us? "But as it is written, 'No eye has seen, nor ear heard, nor the heart of man conceived, what God has prepared for those who love him'" (1 Cor 2:9).

The Eucharist is the pinnacle of Catholic faith. The center and meaning of the Eucharist is the presence of Christ transforming the fruit of the earth (God's Creation) into Himself by His divine will. As we receive the Eucharist in faith and humility, we are likewise transformed by Christ's presence into a new creation. The Eucharist then is awesome to contemplate. Through it, we finite, helpless humans are offered a mystical union with Christ and are allowed as sons and daughters of God to behold the Lamb who was slain for us. Taking into our bodies and souls the Incarnate Christ, the King of Kings, is a monumental event — one that continually transforms our lives.

At the Mass, Catholics hear the Word of God proclaimed in the Holy Scriptures, and this alone would be an incalculable grace. Far beyond this, however, we have the Word made Flesh in the Eucharist. Many have stated that if we really comprehended this mystery, we would run to Mass and crawl up the steps of the church in utter humility for the great gift that has been given to us. In the Eucharist we are made a unique people, set apart for the service of God by the presence of Jesus. In the Gospel of St. John we read these difficult but awe-inspiring words uttered by Christ: "For My flesh is food indeed, and My blood is drink indeed. He who eats My flesh and drinks My blood abides in Me, and I in him" (Jn 6:55–56).

"How can the Eucharist be a sign of eternal life and the world to come unless it is actually the mysterious and Real Presence of Christ in His Body and Blood who comes to us in Holy Communion?

"The whole idea of the Eucharist is that it is a sign that at the end of the ages we shall with our body and soul be united with Christ who is really present to us now with His Body and Blood. 'The death of the Lord' and His return are events that include body and spirit so that the Eucharist we celebrate is not simply spiritual but corporeal. For this reason St. Paul states that in the Eucharist we 'proclaim the Lord's death until he comes' (1 Cor 11:26)."[10]

Quotation for Meditation

The Catholic Church has held on to this faith in the presence in the Eucharist of the Body and Blood of Christ, not only in her teaching but also in her practice, since she has at all times given to this great Sacrament the worship which is known as *Latria* and which may be given to God alone. As St. Augustine says: "It was in His flesh that Christ walked among us and it is His flesh that He has given us to eat for our salvation.

No one, however, eats of this flesh without having first adored it . . . and not only do we not sin in thus adoring but we would sin if we did not do so."

The Catholic Church has always offered and still offers the cult of *Latria* to the sacrament of the Eucharist, not only during Mass, but also outside of it, reserving Consecrated Hosts with the utmost care, exposing them to solemn veneration, and carrying them processionally, to the joy of great crowds of the faithful.

— Pope Paul VI, *Mysterium Fidei* (Mystery of Faith)

❧ Quiet Time and Then Discussion ❧

Questions for Meditation

1. Why is it necessary for Catholics to believe in the miraculous when partaking of the Eucharist?
2. Why is faith in the Eucharistic presence of Christ necessary for the Catholic?
3. What does being a Catholic and receiving the Eucharist mean to you?

Prayer

Lord Jesus Christ, come and be with us throughout the days of our life, and remind us constantly of Your presence by the Holy Eucharist. May we live out in our own lives the events and the meaning of the Last Supper, and may we come at the end of our lives to that great banquet that began that night and that will last through all eternity. Amen.

— Fr. Benedict J. Groeschel, C.F.R.,
The King Crucified and Risen, 134

Meditation Twenty-Three

The Holy Eucharist:
A Royal Banquet

READINGS

Song of Songs 1:12–2:7; John 2:1–10; John 6:48–58;
1 Corinthians 11:27–29; Catechism *1382–1390*

The Lord Jesus prepares an incomparable banquet for His followers at every Mass and has been doing so since the Last Supper. Every time the Eucharist is celebrated, we are issued a royal invitation to an event that has no equal. It doesn't matter where the Mass is celebrated, from an immense Gothic cathedral to a tiny makeshift chapel, the Eucharist is the same; its host is always the King of Kings. The banquet He sets before us has been meticulously prepared down to the smallest of details. No price is demanded of those who are invited — and yet this is a banquet that costs no less than everything; for when we come to the Eucharist, we bring all that we are, down to our innermost secrets. In joy and thanksgiving and profound allegiance to our divine host we surrender everything and allow Him to feed us with Himself. We lose nothing; we gain everything.

Perhaps a little history of the culture of Jesus' time can shed some light on the magnitude and privilege of being invited to such a royal banquet. Kings during biblical times in the Middle East enjoyed absolute dominance over their subjects and lived lives of splendor and luxury. Even very highly placed people rarely were permitted to dine with the king, and on those infrequent occasions when such an honor was permitted, the subjects were made to feel very conscious of their lesser position. The monarch, opulently attired, reclined on a sumptuous couch, eating the richest foods and drinking the finest wines available. The guests, however, had less elegant food and drank an inferior wine while seated upon the floor gazing up at their sovereign.

The Lord who is the host of our banquet, however, is like no other royal host. He is no mere king, president, or dignitary of this world. Our host is unique: He is the Christ, the Messiah, the King of the Jews, the Incarnate Son of God and Mary, the one who redeems us from eternal nothingness. Unlike earthly kings, Jesus prepares the best for His servants. The story of the wedding feast at Cana reminds us that the wine Jesus offers to those He loves is far from inferior; it is immeasurably better than the finest wine men can offer. The royal host of our Eucharistic banquet will never feed us with the food of servants — although that alone would be an immense honor. Instead He feeds us as He would feed His brothers, sisters, friends — as He would feed the heirs to His kingdom.

In the Song of Songs we read of a banquet that beautifully foreshadows the Eucharist. A young bride, ecstatically in love with her groom, says: "He brought me to the banqueting house, and his banner over me was love" (Song 2:4). We can read this book of the Old Testament, in part, as an allegory in which the Church is the mystical bride of Christ and Christ is her eternal bridegroom. For the young lovers in the Song of Songs, love itself is their banner, their deepest reality. It has become their identifying mark, defining them completely. The adoring bridegroom gives his beloved a banquet of the choicest foods the world can offer. In the same way, our adoring bridegroom gives us the Eucharistic banquet in which He offers us His Body, Blood, Soul and Divinity. As Christ makes a gift to us of His deepest reality in the Eucharist, so the love we return to Him must be our deepest reality, as well. It must be our banner, the mark by which the world knows us; it must define us.

A banner can also be a sign of victory, and the Eucharist is an incontrovertible sign of Christ's victory over death and his redemption of mankind. This is beautifully expressed in the opening words of a sixth century hymn for Holy Week: "The royal banners forward go, the cross shines forth in mystic glow, where He whom through our flesh was made in that same flesh our ransom paid."[11] When we attend the royal banquet of the Mass, the one whom death could not conquer comes to us under the triumphant banner of the Eucharist, bringing us the same flesh that ransomed us on the cross, bringing us salvation and abundant life. Despite the awe and humility this enormous gift should instill in us, we must never forget that the Eucharistic banquet is one that should give us great joy and confidence. The joy we feel at the forgiveness of our sins and our acceptance by our divine host should permeate our lives and spill over into everything we do. This joy should be as conspicuous in our lives as a banner boldly unfurled above our heads. It should make all who behold us long to eat at the same royal banquet and to share in what we have been so graciously given.

Quotation for Meditation

O precious and wonderful banquet, that brings us salvation and contains all sweetness! Could anything be of more intrinsic value? Under the old law it was the flesh of calves and goats that was offered but here Christ himself, the true God, is set before us as our food. What could be more wonderful than this? No other sacrament has greater healing power, through it sins are purged away, virtues are increased, and the soul is enriched with an abundance of every spiritual gift. It is offered in the Church for the living and the dead, so that what was instituted for the salvation of all may be for the benefit of all. Yet, in the end, no one can fully express the sweetness of this sacrament, in which spiritual delight is tasted at its very source and in which we renew the memory of that surpassing love for us which Christ revealed in His Passion.

— St. Thomas Aquinas, as cited in
Christian Prayer: The Liturgy of the Hours, 2011

⚜ Quiet Time and Then Discussion ⚜

Questions for Meditation

1. In what way is the Eucharist a banquet?
2. How should we show our joy and celebration for this banquet?
3. How have I responded to God's invitation to the Eucharistic banquet? Do I approach the altar with proper reverence for and understanding of Whom I am about to receive in Communion? What can I do to increase my reverence?

Prayer

Lord, this is thy feast,
prepared by thy longing,
attended at thine invitation,
blessed by thine own Word,
distributed by thine own hand,
the undying memorial of thy sacrifice
upon the Cross,
the full gift of thine everlasting love,
and its perpetuation till time shall end.
Lord, this is Bread of heaven,
Bread of life,
that, whoso eateth, never shall hunger more.
And this the cup of pardon, healing gladness,
*   strength,*
that whoso drinketh, thirsteth not again.
So may we come, O Lord, to thy table,
Lord Jesus, come to us.

— Eric Milner-White, as cited in
The Oxford Book of Prayer, 535

The Fruits of Holy Communion

❧

READINGS
John 6:56–57; 1 Corinthians 10:16–18; Catechism 1391–1401

The *Catechism* teaches us that the principal fruit of receiving the Eucharist is the development of an intimate relationship with our Divine Savior. What food is to the body, the Eucharist is to the spirit. It is the spiritual nourishment we require to grow in Christ as we journey to the Father. The Eucharist preserves us from sin and increases our faith. In it we are given the sacred opportunity to be renewed every day of our lives, to experience the fullness of life in Christ. In the Eucharist we are given food that heals, food that transforms. St. Paul writes: "He who began a good work in you will bring it to completion at the day of Jesus Christ" (Phil 1:6). One way to read these words is as a reference to the Eucharist, which constantly transforms those who receive it, conforming them more and more to Christ.

We are challenged often in this life. Our faults are great; our failures are many. But if we allow Christ to enter deeply into our lives in the Eucharist, we will ultimately know triumph and we will be able to stand with St. Paul, who wrote: "I am not ashamed, for I know whom I have believed, and I am sure that he is able to guard until that Day what has been entrusted to me" (2 Tim 1:12). What has been entrusted to us? Many gifts — among them heavenly food, the very Body and Blood of Our Lord and Savior.

Growth in Christ is inseparable from partaking of the Eucharist. Those who do not receive the Body and Blood of Christ cannot truly know the fullness of life, cannot fully encounter the Divine Redeemer who has given Himself for all mankind. In the reception of the Eucharist, Christ frees us from our sins and brings us from death to new life, making firm our place in His Mystical Body.

At every moment of our lives our heavenly Father is working in countless ways to bring us to salvation. His grace, however, is made available in special ways through the sacraments. Through these sacred mysteries, God reaches out to us, bestowing upon us the grace to turn from sin and selfishness and accept the divine love. We receive most of the sacraments only once, but to the sacraments of Reconciliation and the Eucharist we return over and over again to be made whole when we are broken, to be forgiven when we have sinned, to be united with Christ when we have abandoned Him for the temptations of a God-starved world. These two sacraments are vital for each of us. Without them we will eventually dwell in spiritual emptiness. They are special medicine that is always available to heal our sin-battered souls and strengthen us to begin the journey again and again.

St. Peter wrote: "Be sober, be watchful, your adversary the devil prowls around like a roaring lion, seeking someone to devour" (1 Pet 5:8). Peter knew what it was to surrender to temptation; he deserted Jesus at the hour of Our Lord's greatest need and denied Him three times out of fear. Yet he also knew forgiveness and newness of life. Through the acceptance of God's grace on Pentecost, Peter was transformed from a terrified man who was concerned only with his own safety into the first pope who courageously proclaimed the Good News of Jesus Christ and who met martyrdom with serenity and faith. The devil sought to sift Peter like a kernel of wheat, but God's grace prevailed. If our commitment to the Eucharist and to Reconciliation remain firm, we too will be transformed. If we regularly take the Body, Blood, Soul, and Divinity of Jesus Christ into our souls through the Eucharist, we, too, will finally know the serenity that Peter experienced. If we permit the fruits of the Eucharist to grow in our lives, we will find open to us the one path that leads to true joy.

Quotation for Meditation

"This body even when lying in the manger the Magi reverenced. Heathen and foreign men left their country and their home, and went [on] a long journey, and came and worshipped Him with fear and much trembling. Let us then, the citizens of heaven, imitate these foreigners. For they approached with great awe when they saw Him in the manger and in the cell, and saw Him in no way such as thou dost see Him now. For thou dost see Him not in a manger but on an altar, not with a woman holding Him but with a priest standing before Him, and the Spirit descending upon the offerings with great bounty. . . . For as in the palaces of Kings what is most splendid of all is not the walls, or the golden roof, but the body of the King sitting on the throne, so also in heaven there is the body of the King; but this thou mayest now behold on earth. For I show to thee not angels, nor archangels, nor the heaven, nor the heaven of heavens, but Him who is the Lord of these Himself."

— St. John Chrysostom's Homily 24 on 1 Corinthians, no. 5, as cited in *In the Presence of Our Lord*, 179

ᘖ Quiet Time and Then Discussion ᘗ

Questions for Meditation

1. How does the Eucharist help us to develop intimacy with Christ?
2. How can I better prepare myself to receive the Eucharist in order to strengthen my walk with Christ?
3. In what way is growth in Christ inseparable from partaking in the Eucharist?

Prayer

Almighty and ever-living God,
I approach the sacrament of your only-begotten Son
our Lord Jesus Christ.
I come sick to the doctor of life,
unclean to the fountain of mercy,
blind to the radiance of eternal light,
and poor and needy to the Lord of heaven and earth.
Lord, in your great generosity,
heal my sickness, wash away my defilement,
enlighten my blindness, enrich my poverty,
and clothe my nakedness.
May I receive the bread of angels

the King of Kings and the Lord of Lords,
with humble reverence,
with the purity and faith,
the repentance and love, and the determined purpose
that will help to bring me to salvation.
May I receive the sacrament of the Lord's Body and Blood,
and its reality and power.
Kind God,
may I receive the Body of Your only-begotten Son,
our Lord Jesus Christ,
born from the womb of the Virgin Mary,
and so be received into his mystical Body,
and numbered among his members,
Loving Father,
as on my earthly pilgrimage
I now receive your beloved Son
under the veil of a sacrament,
may I one day see him face to face in glory,
who lives and reigns with you for ever. Amen.

— St. Thomas Aquinas,
as cited in the *Vatican II Sunday Missal*

The Pledge of the Glory to Come

❧

READINGS
Matthew 28:19, 20; John 14:15–18; Catechism *1402–1419*

The second coming of Christ is an event that we can anticipate with confidence. No one may know the precise hour when the Son of God will come at the end of time, but what we do know for certain is that He comes to us at every Mass. Therefore, the Eucharist is a pledge of Christ's return to us in glory.

The Lord Jesus came in His first Advent as a baby born of a virgin. He became an itinerant preacher, a worker of wonders who eventually gave Himself over to suffering and death. When, in the eyes of the world all was lost, He rose again as the Divine Messiah who would never again experience the grave. In His life, death and resurrection, Jesus Christ fulfilled thousands of years of prophecy and demonstrated in the most profound way possible God's infinite love for those He has created.

The Lord promised never to leave us, never to forsake us. In the Eucharist Christ fulfills that divine promise in a way no human mind could have anticipated. The God who came to us as a helpless child in Bethlehem now comes to us under the appearances of bread and wine. Unlike Jesus' original disciples, we neither have to await the Last Supper nor experience the horrors of Good Friday. We can encounter the Risen Christ every day at Mass. In the Eucharist we have our Divine Redeemer in our lives, guiding us in union with the Father and the Holy Spirit. We have in the great gift of the Eucharist God's pledge of undying love for us despite our sinfulness, despite our constant turning away from Him.

In faith and confidence the Church continues to await Christ's second coming, but there are countless people who cannot bring themselves to believe in it at all, just as there are many who do not believe that He returns to us in the Eucharist. Numerous Protestants and even Catholics struggle to accept these teachings or reject them outright. This is a sad state of affairs, of course, but why should it surprise us? Many walked away from Jesus during His earthly life. Despite the signs and wonders He worked, there were those who found His words too difficult, too challenging. Their lives were too comfortable for them to be willing to risk everything on the extravagant promises of a carpenter's son — even one who healed the sick and restored life to the dead.

Are we like those people who turned away from the Incarnate Son of God as He walked the dusty roads of ancient Palestine? Are our lives too comfortable to allow us to risk all by accepting this Christ Whose promises are no less extravagant today than they were two thousand years ago? When we receive the Eucharist do we really believe that Christ enters our very being, that in it we have Jesus' pledge of the eternal glory that will one day be ours? Or does part of us remain unmoved, skeptical? Do we try to find a way to rationalize what is impossible to understand, to turn the Eucharist into something that fits neatly into some human pattern of thought? Could there be a deeply hidden part of us that finds it impossible to believe in a God who loves us so much that He gave His only begotten Son for us?

But even if we struggle to accept these truths, there is cause for joy, for the struggle itself shows that God's grace is at work within us. Even the greatest saints had periods of profound darkness and doubt. Through perseverance and the grace of God, however, they triumphed, and so shall we. Therefore, in our moments of uncertainty and doubt we turn to Christ again and again. We renew our prayer life; we participate in the Mass; we contemplate the Eucharist until finally we come to sense a tiny fraction of its reality and begin to know it as God's great pledge to us of His infinite love.

As the Lord rained down manna from heaven on the Israelites in the desert, He brings Himself to His children every day in the Eucharist. Let us be eternally thankful for this great gift and may we pray that one day all mankind will turn to the God who once humbled Himself to be born in a manger and who daily humbles Himself to come to His sinful creatures under the forms of bread and wine. Let us pray that all will finally acknowledge Christ's pledge of eternal glory to us that is made real in the Eucharist.

Quotation for Meditation

On his way to martyrdom, St. Ignatius of Antioch proclaimed: "I am God's grain, and I am being ground by the teeth of wild beasts in order that I may be found [to be] pure bread for Christ. My [earthly] love [lit. *eros*] has been crucified, and there is in me no fire of material love, but rather a living water, speaking in me and saying within me, 'Come to the Father.' I take no pleasure in corruptible food or in the delights of this life. I want the Bread of God, which is the Flesh of Jesus Christ, who is of the seed of David; and as drink I want his Blood, which is incorruptible love."
— Msgr. James O'Connor,
The Hidden Manna: A Theology of the Eucharist, 13

∾ Quiet Time and Then Discussion ∾

Questions for Meditation

1. How strong is my faith in the Eucharist, and how can I increase it?
2. Why should we believe the Lord is coming in glory?
3. What are my secret doubts, and how can I surrender them to draw closer to Christ in the Eucharist?

Prayer

Lord Jesus, on the Road to Emmaus You made Yourself known to Your disciples in the Breaking of the Bread. I ask the same gift for myself. Grant me the grace to know You in the bread that is no longer bread but Your Holy Body; grant me the grace never to overlook You in the wine that is no longer wine but Your Blood outpoured. Let me approach every Holy Communion aware of Whom I go to meet. Let me encounter You fully at the altar despite my many sins, and let me never fail to welcome You with love into my soul. Lord Jesus, be known to me in the Breaking of the Bread. Amen.

Meditation Twenty-Six

The Sacrament of Reconciliation

READINGS
*Isaiah 53:4–10; Ezekiel 36:23–26; Matthew 11:28–30;
John 10:1–6; Catechism 1420–1424*

The sacrament of Reconciliation ought to give us great joy, for it is a sacrament of healing. Like all sacraments, it flows directly from the atoning work of Christ on Calvary. In Isaiah 53:5, we read: "He was wounded for our transgressions, he was bruised for our iniquities; upon him was the chastisement that made us whole, and with his stripes we are healed." Thus spiritual and physical healing are implicit in our Divine Savior's great sacrifice on Good Friday, healing that even now continues to stream forth abundantly from the wounded side of Christ.

Sacred Scripture often likens mankind to sheep who have gone astray, and indeed, much of Scripture records tales of people straying from God in a seemingly endless assortment of ways. All such straying, however, can be reduced to a rejection of our heavenly Father and a free embrace of sin. Sheep may be very gentle animals, but they are not noted for their intelligence. They have many limitations and are in great need of a shepherd to save them from outside dangers as well as from their own mistakes. Sheep will graze on the side of a mountain, eating the grass down to the root until not a blade is left. They will stay there until someone guides them to the other side of the mountain where fresh grass is abundant. It is not surprising that we are told we are like sheep, we who cause so much of our own unhappiness and so often become hopelessly mired in our own mistakes.

When we come to confess our sins in the sacrament of Reconciliation, our spirits are often dry, desolate. We are like the sheep who have been trying to graze on the barren side of the mountain. We are starving for spiritual nourishment and have tried unsuccessfully to obtain such sustenance from meaningless distractions and diversions. Perhaps we have given our allegiance to some idol that cannot truly sustain us, such as money, power, or sexuality. Perhaps our souls dwell in the dark despair of mortal sin. But when we sincerely confess our sins, we do not encounter the retribution of a stern king; we find instead the gentle acceptance of a faithful shepherd. In infinite love and perfect justice, God frees us from our sins and satisfies our spiritual emptiness with His abundant graces. He brings us back to His fold, rejoicing in our return. He quenches our thirst with living waters. He gives us renewed life.

We who have experienced the sacrament of Reconciliation have known the love of God in an unmatched way. In this sacrament we receive an assurance of our Father's love for us. We are reminded that our heavenly shepherd is always there to forgive if we but turn to Him in genuine repentance. As we contemplate the great gift of the sacrament of Reconciliation, we are reminded of Christ's compassion recorded in Matthew 9:36: "But when he saw the multitudes he had compassion for them, because they were harassed and helpless, like sheep without a shepherd."

No matter how many times we stray into sin, we must never lose hope, for we have among us one who represents our heavenly shepherd. In joy and thanksgiving we should run to the priest who hears our confession and administers, *in persona Christi*, God's healing grace, and we should never fail to rejoice in God's forgiveness and reconciliation.

Quotation for Meditation

The scorpion's bite is venomous, but from its substance is extracted a remedy which heals that very bite: so our sins are shameful when we commit them, but when they are turned to confession and penitence they are a source of spiritual benefit and welfare. Contrition and confession are so lovely and acceptable that they efface the stain and disperse the stench of the sin.

Simon the leper called the Magdalen a sinner, but our Savior spoke not of her sins, but only of the precious ointment which she poured out, and of the fullness of her love. If we are truly humble . . . we shall grieve bitterly over our sin because it offends God, but we shall find sweetness in accusing ourselves, because in doing so we honor Him; and we shall find relief in fully revealing our complaints to our physician. When you are before your spiritual father, suppose you are on Mount Calvary, at the feet of the crucified Jesus, whose Precious Blood drops upon you to purify your iniquities. For although it is no longer His very Blood, nevertheless, it is the virtue of His Bloodshedding, which so plentifully descends upon the penitent in the confessional. Hesitate not then to open your heart fully in confession, for in proportion as your sins go forth, the precious merits of Christ's Passion will come in and fill you with all blessings.

— St. Francis de Sales,
An Introduction to the Devout Life, 44

Quiet Time and Then Discussion

Questions for Meditation

1. From what does the sacrament of Reconciliation ultimately flow?

2. What are the secret idols I worship in my own life, and how can I use the sacrament of Reconciliation to rid myself of my enslavement to them?

3. In this meditation, people are compared to sheep. In what ways do I act like a sheep, and how can I change my life to become more of the person God intended me to be?

Prayer

God and Father of our Lord Jesus Christ,
though your people walk in the valley of darkness,
no evil should they fear;
for they follow in faith the call of the shepherd
whom you have sent for their hope and strength.
Attune our minds to the sound of his voice,
lead our steps in the path he has shown,
that we may know the strength of his outstretched arm
and enjoy the light of your presence for ever.
We ask this in the name of Jesus the Lord. Amen.

— Alternative Opening Prayer
for the Fourth Sunday of Easter

Meditation Twenty-Seven

The Sacrament of Reconciliation:
A Path to Ongoing Conversion

❧

READINGS
Romans 7:14–25; Mark 1:15;
Catechism *1425–1429*

Our lives can be described in many ways. Perhaps one of the most realistic of these is to say that they are journeys of ongoing conversion. From the moment we become aware of God, we also become aware that no matter how we try, we fall short in our relationship with God. We try to love, but we fail. We try to be generous, but we're selfish. We try to turn our backs on sin, but somehow we end up running toward it instead. Our conversion to God is always a process — usually a difficult and sometimes painful one. It will never be complete until we leave this world and rest in God's eternal changelessness.

St. Paul's conversion was about as dramatic as is possible for a human being to undergo and still survive. Thrown to the ground by a blinding vision of Christ, he finds his whole world transformed. All that he has believed is changed. He has but one concern now — an obsession really — and that is Christ. His name is even changed from Saul to Paul because he has encountered the divine presence and can never again be the same. But he still sins. In his letter to the Romans he laments this in frustration and bewilderment: "We know that the Law is spiritual; but I am carnal, sold under sin. I do not understand my own actions. For I do not do what I want, but I do the very thing that I hate" (Rom 7:14,15). Even after his experience on the road to Damascus, Paul is still in need of constant forgiveness, of reconciliation, of conversion. If this is so for St. Paul, what must it be like for the rest of us?

Human nature is frail, enfeebled by the effects of original sin. It is weakened still further by the many actual sins we commit and the patterns of sin in which we live so much of our earthly lives. If the human race were left to its own devices, only one person who ever lived would find her way to God — Mary, the Mother of God. We are in need of constant help, constant conversion and reconversion. Without it we are lost. But such help is graciously given to us. It is in the sacrament of Reconciliation that we find an endless supply of such help, for Reconciliation has as its inexhaustible source our Savior's sacrifice on Calvary, the most complete and perfect act of reconciliation possible.

As Catholics, we are realists. We know our propensity to sin; we know our love of the very things we should avoid. Despite this, however, we should be joyful.

For hope is given us. We fall again and again, but we return again and again to the wellspring of grace that is the sacrament of Reconciliation. Days pass; years vanish; and still we continue to revisit this great sacrament and are forgiven anew. If we stand firm in this, if we do not lose hope, we will one day see a change in ourselves. As the grace of Reconciliation enters more and more deeply into our lives, it slowly begins to bear fruit. It reconfigures us to Christ. It makes us into the people God created us to be.

Quotation for Meditation

"The choice of Christ in the concreteness of daily living that is marked by the battle between good and evil cannot but assume the face of conversion: a conversion of the intellect, by virtue of which the Lord becomes the ultimate and definitive criterion by which life is judged; and the conversion of natural instinct so as to become able to love in order to give and not to possess.

In support of this conversion, the Lord instituted the sacrament of Reconciliation. In it, Christ Himself reaches out to meet man who is oppressed by the awareness of his own weakness, lifts him up from his prostration and gives him the necessary strength to resume his journey. In this sacrament it is the life of the risen Christ which is poured into the soul of the believer, giving rise to renewed generosity of intention in the enthusiasm of a more convinced fidelity to His Gospel."

— Pope John Paul II,
Walk According to the Spirit, 98

Quiet Time and Then Discussion

Questions for Meditation

1. What weakens human nature and makes it easy for us to fall into sin?
2. How is your own life a process of ongoing conversion?
3. What helps and what hinders us in ongoing conversion?

THE SACRAMENT OF RECONCILIATION: A PATH TO ONGOING CONVERSION

Prayer

Lord Jesus,
you chose to be called the friend of sinners.
By your saving death and resurrection,
free me from my sins.
May peace take root in my heart
and bring forth a harvest
of love, holiness, and truth. Amen.

— From the *Rite of Penance*

Interior Penance

Sincere interior penance is necessary if our faith is to grow. One who perseveres in seeking interior penance, who genuinely attempts reconciliation and amendment of life, will develop in faith. This usually happens slowly, even imperceptibly. For most of us it is a process that takes a lifetime — but it happens. A sincere admission of our sins, our faults and failings, flaws and misdeeds in the presence of a priest opens to us God's boundless torrent of graces, enabling us to change. Through true penance and reconciliation we receive what the psalmist yearned for so desperately when he pleaded: "Create in me a clean heart, O God, and renew a right spirit within me" (Ps 51). The true penitent is one who admits his inadequacies before God, who — like the psalmist — knows that it is God's grace and not his own strivings alone that will bring him to transformation. True penance cultivates the human heart, making it a fertile place for God to plant seeds of faith. Penance can break through the driest soil of our hearts and cause to bloom within us a garden of the fruit of the Holy Spirit. Through true penance we can obtain the things that St. Paul describes in his letter to the Galatians: "... the fruit of the Spirit is love, joy, peace, patience, kindness, goodness, faithfulness, gentleness, self-control; against such there is no law. And those who belong to Christ Jesus have crucified the flesh with its passions and desires" (Gal 5:22–24).

Interior penance helps us control our negative passions and causes our hearts to burn with increased longing for God. Penance enables us to resist the culture of death, to choose life instead. Step by slow step, penance removes the callousness from a heart that has resisted God until that heart finally turns to the Lord without reservation. The penitent soul relentlessly pushes toward God like the woman with the hemorrhage of whom we read in the Gospels. Despite the fact that Jesus was surrounded by throngs of people and despite the fact that she must have been very weak because of her illness, the woman thrusts herself forward again and again, until finally she is able to touch the hem of Jesus' garment. At that moment, she is cured. "Courage, my daughter," Jesus says to her. "Your faith has made you well" (Lk 8:48). This determined faith-filled woman is a model for us as we cultivate interior penance. She shows us the fruits of faith. She demonstrates the necessity of perseverance.

In the beloved Twenty-Third Psalm we read: "Surely goodness and mercy shall follow me all the days of my life; and I shall dwell in the house of the Lord forever" (Ps 23:6). The psalmist here has experienced in his own life the power of a penitent heart and God's forgiveness. His fears — even of the valley of the shadow of death — are made manageable by his faith in God. This faith inexorably leads to confidence and to a joy so great that it fills his cup to the point of overflowing.

There is no substitute in the spiritual life for developing a penitent heart. To do this, we must abandon faith in ourselves and turn instead in faith and trust to the one "from whom all good things come," for conversion of heart depends ultimately on God's grace. May our lives be ones that continually yield to the call of penance and reconciliation until we find that our cup overflows with joy.

Quotation for Meditation

Never forget, then: every time you receive [the] sacrament [of Reconciliation] worthily, with devotion, even if there are only venial sins to confess, the Blood of Christ flows in abundance upon your soul, so as to vivify it, make it strong against temptation, render it generous in the struggle against attachment to sin;

and so as to destroy in it the roots and the effects of sin. The soul finds in this sacrament a special grace for uprooting vices and purifying itself more and more; for regaining the life of grace or increasing that life within itself.

Before confession, then, let us always renew our faith in the infinite value of the expiation made by Jesus Christ. He has borne the weight of all our sins, He has been offered for each one of us: He "loved me and gave Himself up for me." His satisfactions are more than superabundant; He has won the right to pardon us; there is no sin that cannot be wiped out by His Divine Blood.

— Blessed Columba Marmion,
Christ, the Life of the Soul, 248

✎ Quiet Time and Then Discussion ✎

Questions for Meditation

1. What reverses our negative passions and desires?
2. How can we turn from sin and develop a penitent heart?
3. What prevents us from embracing sincere interior penance in our own lives?

Prayer

*Lord Jesus Christ, Son of God,
have mercy on me, a sinner.*

Meditation Twenty-Nine

A Bridge to God

READINGS
1 John 1:8–10 and 2:12; John 3:16–18; Catechism 1440–1449

Sin enters human life early. The book of Genesis is barely begun before we encounter mankind's first sin, one of a long catalogue of offenses that leads to greater and greater disaster. Adam and Eve have been created for a life of happiness. God has given them everything they could want — and more — for He has given them His divine presence. He is their loving companion as they walk through the Garden of Eden. Yet even this is not enough. They envy the one who created them and yearn to be equal to Him. This longing leads them to transgression and sin and costs them the divine presence and the perfect world for which they had been created.

We are all Adams and Eves who yearn to be our own gods. We put our heavenly Father's law aside and replace it with one of our own devising. It is our will, not God's, that must be done. In the biblical account of the Garden of Eden, we encounter the original sin that afflicts every soul and darkens every life. We learn that from the very beginning our sin has caused a rupture in the one relationship that can bring us joy and life. Despite the tragedy of sin and its utter pervasiveness, however, there is cause not only for hope, but for great rejoicing. In the words of St. John's Gospel: "The light shines in the darkness and the darkness has not overcome it" (Jn 1:5). Out of love for sinful man, the Second Person of the Blessed Trinity comes to us as our Messiah, to live as one of us, to die for us and to restore us to the presence of God.

As Catholic Christians, we have the great consolation of knowing that we are offered constant regeneration and sanctification through the redeeming power of Jesus Christ. We are aware that the sacraments are the primary means through which such grace is dispensed to us, and we know that Reconciliation is the sacrament through which God works in a special way to heal our fallen nature. In this wonderful sacrament our heavenly Father rids us of our sins as if they are so much excess baggage. The writer of the letter to the Hebrews uses a similar metaphor when he writes: ". . . let us lay aside every weight and sin which clings so closely, and let us run with perseverance the race which is set before us, looking to Jesus the pioneer and perfecter of our faith, who for the joy that was set before him endured the cross, despising the shame and is seated at the right hand of the throne of God" (Heb 12: 1–2).

We remember that we are redeemed through no effort of our own, but by God's love. Nonetheless, as we journey to the Father, we must be God's willing cooperators in our own ultimate salvation. We must commit ourselves to overcoming sin in all ways and at all times. To do this, we must approach the sacrament of Reconciliation with regularity and sincerity. In so doing, we gradually root out the sins that darken our lives; we slowly overcome our pride, our envy, and our selfishness; we are made able to accept God's healing graces deeply into our souls until at last we are ready to walk with the divine presence once again.

Quotation for Meditation

"The whole of the Christian life is like a great *pilgrimage to the house of the Father*, whose unconditional love for every human creature, and in particular for the 'prodigal son' (cf. Lk 15:11–32), we discover anew each day. This pilgrimage takes place in the heart of each person, extends to the believing community, and then reaches to the whole of humanity."

— Pope John Paul II, *Tertio Millennio Adveniente*
(As the Third Millenniium Draws Near), 49

✺ Quiet Time and Then Discussion ✺

Questions for Meditation

1. How is the sacrament of Reconciliation a primary help to the healing of our fallen nature?

2. How is the collaboration with God carried out in our daily lives in a personal way as members in a church?

3. Despite our many sins, why is it that we never have cause to lose heart?

Prayer

Father of mercy,
like the prodigal son
I return to you and say:
"I have sinned against you
and am no longer worthy to be called your son."
Christ Jesus, Savior of the world,
I pray with the repentant thief
to whom you promised Paradise:
"Lord, remember me in your kingdom."
Holy Spirit, fountain of love,
I call on you with trust:
"Purify my heart,
and help me walk as a child of light."
Amen.

— From the *Rite of Penance*

The Joy of Repentance

✑

READINGS
Isaiah 1:16–19; Luke 15:11–32;
Catechism *1450–1460*

The Christian life is one lived in constant repentance. Perhaps that statement seems somehow dreary, discouraging, daunting. But it shouldn't. If we have a true understanding of repentance, we know that it means to turn. As we turn from one thing we find ourselves turning toward something else. In turning from sin, what we turn toward is our heavenly Father. Could there be greater cause for joy?

The sacrament of Reconciliation is a great gift in this regard. It reinforces our willingness to turn from evil and to conform our will to the will of the Father. It enables us to put aside our selfishness, our frantic, laughable efforts to control others, to impose our human will on all things — even God. It enables us to submit in faith and trust to the one who spread out the heavens and established the earth, whose love sustains our existence from instant to instant.

As the time of His Passion and death drew near, Our Lord Jesus Christ underwent His Agony in the Garden of Gethsemane. Even as the dread anticipation of Good Friday convulsed His human nature in terror, He was able to cry out: "My Father, if it be possible, let this cup of suffering pass from me; nevertheless, not as I will, but as thou wilt" (Mt 26:39). In the darkness of the Garden of Gethsemane, and at all times during His earthly life, Jesus submitted perfectly to the will of the Father. In that submission mankind was brought to salvation. The regular and sincere use of the sacrament of Reconciliation increases in us the kind of faith that enables us — at least at times — to submit to God's mysterious will, to be like Jesus and make real those difficult words of the Lord's Prayer: "Thy will be done."

We each face our private Gethsemanes, powerful challenges to faith that shake us to the very core of our being, that cause us to doubt, that push us toward despair. Sometimes God seems hidden, unreachable, impossibly distant — absent. But even at these times God has not abandoned us any more than God abandoned Jesus in His agony on Holy Thursday evening. We have the sacraments of Reconciliation and the Eucharist as unending pledges of God's presence and love. They enable us to turn. In them we find the strength to say — however tentatively — "not as I will, but as thou wilt."

As we turn more and more to God and away from sin, we become like the godly man extolled in Psalm 1:3: "He is like a tree planted by streams of water, that yields its fruit in its season, and its leaf does not wither. In all that he does, he prospers." In these words we see what truly happens when we live in conformity to the will of God. This spiritual prosperity is the result of a life that constantly turns away from sin and toward the Father, that has been strengthened by Reconciliation and nourished by the Eucharist. This is a life that is lived in the joy of repentance.

Quotation for Meditation

God places His glory in relieving our misery in forgiving our sins. God wills to be glorified by showing His mercy towards us, because of the satisfactions of His beloved Son. In eternity, says St. John, we shall sing a hymn to God and to the Lamb. And what will that hymn be? Will it be the *Holy, Holy, Holy* of the angels? God did not spare one faction of His pure spirits: after their first revolt, He struck like a thunderbolt cast them out — because they had not those weaknesses, those miseries that are our lot. The faithful angels sing of the holiness of God — that holiness which could not have suffered the defection of the rebels for one instant.

But we — what will *our* hymn be? One that sings of mercy: "The mercies of the Lord I will sing for ever." That verse of the Psalmist will be like a refrain of the hymn of love we shall sing to God. We shall sing it also to the Lamb. And what is it that we shall sing to Him? "You have redeemed us, Lord, by your Blood"— you have redeemed us by your precious Blood to save us from our miseries, to free us from our sins; it is what here below in the Mass is said every day in Your name: "This is the chalice of my Blood which has been shed for the remission of sins."

Yes, immense glory returns to God from this mercy He exercises towards sinners who claim upon the satisfactions of His Son Jesus. Whence, it can be understood that one of the greatest affronts that could be made to God is doubting His mercy and the pardon He gives us in Jesus Christ.

—Blessed Columba Marmion,
Christ, the Life of the Soul, 244

❧ Quiet Time and Then Discussion ❧

Questions for Meditation

1. What is the basic meaning of the word repentance?
2. What reinforces our willingness to turn from evil?

3. What are the things that make it especially difficult in your life to submit to God's will?

Prayer

Almighty Father,
For one thing alone do I pray,
that You renew my will from day to day,
that you blend it with thine and take away
all that now makes it hard to say,
"Thy will be done."
Amen.

Meditation Thirty-One

God's Gift of Healing

$\backsim$

READINGS
Isaiah 35:1–6; Psalm 91; John 10:27–28; Catechism 1499–1513

O ur contemporary culture — so terrified of death — is obsessed with health and ways to preserve it. We eat health foods and join health clubs. Maintaining proper health insurance for ourselves and our families is imperative. Annually, our universities produce armies of confident young physicians whose training becomes ever more technical, specialized, and expensive. Our hospitals are temples of technology, and we are convinced they will save us from all forms of illness, from the passage of time, from mortality. And when traditional medicine fails us, we run to alternative practitioners who promise us wholeness and offer us the wisdom of ancient China and India, who treat us with herbs and incantations, with vitamins and strange nutritional regimes.

But all our frenzied efforts are doomed, for we are human and will eventually fall victim to our own humanity. Illness or the infirmities of age will inevitably touch us, and force us to acknowledge what we labor so unceasingly to ignore. In the words of the *Catechism*: "Every illness can make us glimpse death" (CCC 1500).

All life is a journey toward death and the existence that lies beyond the moment when we close our eyes for the last time. All life is a journey toward the source of life, a return to the One Who alone can offer us real health, Who alone can bind our many wounds and make us whole. To aid us in our journey, Christ offers us uncountable gifts if we but open our eyes to see them, unending ways to find peace as we make our journey, as we confront illness, loss, and mortality. The sacraments are the most crucial among these gifts, and the one that the divine love has provided to us in times of illness is the Anointing of the Sick. In this great sacrament, the infinite saving power of God is bestowed upon us. Through this sacrament this power is brought directly into our lives, into our very being. The Old Testament is filled with stories of the healing power of the God of Israel. In these stories, a healing of the soul accompanies a healing of the body. A conversion, a deepening of the relationship between the one who heals and the one who is healed is invariably part of a return to physical health. The New Testament is a virtual catalogue of the unstoppable healing power of Jesus. The lame, the blind, the bleeding, the leprous, the possessed, all find healing in Jesus, and they find it easily, without cost. Jesus bestows it freely and happily. Healing bursts forth from Him, like light from the sun. One has but to touch the hem of His garment to experience it. In these stories, too, we encounter a healing far deeper than a mere return to physical health. Faith is built; sin is abandoned; peace is given; the eternal soul is healed along with the perishable body.

Such healing is available to us today. We can encounter the same Jesus, the same Risen Christ, in the sacrament of the Anointing of the Sick. This sacrament is described in the Letter of St. James: "Is any among you sick? Let him call for the elders of the church, and let them pray over him, anointing him with oil in the name of the Lord; and the prayer of faith will save the sick man, and the Lord will raise him up; and if he has committed sins he will be forgiven" (Jas 5:13–15). In these words we are assured of a type of healing which makes modern medicine seem insignificant. In them we encounter the healing power of God, which transforms the catastrophe of being human into victory.

Quotation for Meditation

Souls who walk in light sing the hymns of light; those who walk in the shadows chant the hymns of darkness. Each must be allowed to sing through to the end the words and melody which God has given him. Nothing must be changed in what he has composed. Every drop of distress, bitter as gall though it may be, must be allowed o flow, no matter what its effect on us. It was the same for Jeremiah and Ezekiel, whose every utterance was broken by sighs and tears. They found consolation only in continuing their laments. Had their tears been halted, we should have lost the loveliest passages in Scripture. The spirit which makes us suffer is the only one which can comfort us. These different waters flow from the same source. If God seems angry, we tremble; if He threatens us, we are terrified. But we can only let the divine project develop, for within itself it contains both the disease and its cure.

— Jean-Pierre de Caussade, S.J.,
Abandonment to Divine Providence, 101

Quiet Time and Then Discussion

Questions for Meditation

1. What does the *Catechism* tell us we can glimpse in every severe illness?
2. In Scripture, what usually accompanies healing?
3. Of what should the sacrament of the Anointing of the Sick constantly remind us?

Prayer

I will extol thee, O LORD,
for thou hast drawn me up,
and hast not let my foes rejoice
over me.
O LORD my God, I cried to thee for
help,
and thou hast healed me.
O LORD thou hast brought up my soul
from Sheol,
restored me to life from among
those gone down to the Pit.

— Psalm 30:1–3

God's Healing Is Available to All

~~~

READINGS
Jeremiah 17:14; Hebrews 4:14–16; Mark 6:7–13;
Catechism *1514–1516*

Severe illness is one of life's great traumas. During such illness we are confronted with our own weakness, our mortality, our ultimate inability to save ourselves. Illness often puts us into the hands of others, making us totally dependent on our doctors, our nurses, our caregivers. We feel we have become less than what we once were, that our humanity is somehow slipping from our grasp. We feel terrifyingly alone.

The sacrament of the Anointing of the Sick is God's great gift to the ill, no matter what form their infirmity may take. In the Anointing of the Sick, we are reminded that it is God's hands in which we truly rest, that all healing — like all life— comes not from strangers but from our heavenly Father. In this sacrament we encounter the Divine Physician who yearns to make us whole, who loves us regardless of our infirmities. This is the God who will never permit illness to make us less than He created us to be, the God who will never let our humanity slip from His grasp or abandon us to lonely, terrifying anguish. Therefore, this sacrament is not limited to those who are in imminent danger of death but is available to all who are ill of body, mind, or spirit. It is a sacrament that can be repeated as it is needed, and the Church urges us to make use of it as a primary means of receiving God's healing graces.

At almost every Mass, we are called upon to pray for the sick and the dying during the Prayer of the Faithful. We know that it is one of the great duties of the members of the Church to be in constant prayer for all people throughout the world, including the sick. It goes without saying that the intercession of the saints is regularly invoked by those in search of healing. All this reminds us that it is the divine will that the prayers of the entire Mystical Body of Christ be constantly and intimately bound up with the dispensation of His healing graces. Yet it is the sacrament of the Anointing of the Sick that was established by Christ as a unique pathway to those graces. This sacrament, of course, can be administered only by those in Holy Orders. Therefore, when we face significant illness of any kind, we should ask for the prayers of others, of course, but we should quickly go to the one among us who stands *in persona Christi* and request the sacrament in which we encounter the Divine Physician whose power, like his love, knows no bounds.

Quotation for Meditation

Let nothing trouble you,
let nothing frighten you.
All things are passing;
God never changes.
Patience obtains all things.
He who possesses God lacks nothing:
God alone suffices.

— St. Teresa of Ávila

❧ Quiet Time and Then Discussion ❧

Questions for Meditation

1. Who can receive the Anointing of the Sick?
2. How often may one receive this sacrament?
3. In what way does the sacrament of the Anointing of the Sick differ from other prayers for healing?

Prayer

Dear Lord, you are the great physician. I turn to you in my sickness and ask you to help me. Put your hand upon me as you did for people long ago and let health and wholeness come into me from you. I put myself under your care and affirm my faith that even now your marvelous healing grace is making me well and strong again. I know that I ask more than I deserve, but you never measure our benefits on that basis. You just love us back into health. Do that for me, I earnestly ask, and I will try to serve you more faithfully. This I promise through Christ our Lord. Amen.

— Terence Cardinal Cooke, *Prayers for Today*, 54

Meditation Thirty-Three

The Benefits of the Anointing
of the Sick

⊘

READINGS
Psalm 145:14–22; Matthew 11:25–30;
Catechism *1520–1523*

The effects of serious illness are never just physical; they spill over into every aspect of life, affecting us in profound ways both psychologically and spiritually. During a severe illness, one is often at the mercy of a torrent of conflicting feelings, a roller coaster of emotions that may be difficult to understand and impossible to control.

At such a time of confusion and anguish we are often tempted to waiver in our trust and confidence in God. We feel abandoned by our heavenly Father. Meaning seems to drain from life, and all becomes darkness. Angrily, we demand an answer to the question that on our side of the grave can have no answer: "Why?"

But the sacrament of the Anointing of the Sick reminds us that we are not alone, that the divine help is with us. In the words of the *Catechism*, "The first grace of the sacrament is one of strengthening, peace and courage to overcome the difficulties that go with the condition of serious illness or the frailty of old age. This grace is a gift of the Holy Spirit, who renews trust and faith in God and strengthens against the temptations of the evil one, the temptation to discouragement and anguish . . ." (CCC 1520).

Whether the sacrament of the Anointing of the Sick cures us or not, it still heals. It heals our souls through the forgiveness of our sins; it heals our minds by bringing us the divine comfort; it heals the world by giving us the immeasurable gift of participating in Christ's work: It enables us to unite our sufferings with His for the good of all. This sacrament can make real in our lives St. Paul's famous but mysterious words: "I fill up in my flesh what is still lacking in regard to Christ's afflictions, for the sake of his Body, which is the Church" (Col 1:24).

Quotation for Meditation

"I think of the great example of my friend Terence Cardinal Cooke, who struggled silently with cancer for almost a decade. My memory recalls a whole kaleidoscope of scenes — him standing in the rain to greet the people after Mass only a week after he received his terminal diagnosis (unbeknown to us all), his patient concern for his critics, his merciful forgiveness of his enemies, his freedom from a vindictive spirit, and his consistent interest in the welfare of those in trouble. His terminal period should have been half as long as it was, his last months should have been a time of gradual deterioration, but he worked consistently for the good of the Church and of all who lived in his sphere of influence. During the last few weeks of his life he divided his time between long periods of prayer and writing letters on very serious issues like life and world peace."

— Fr. Benedict J. Groeschel, C.F.R.,
Arise from Darkness, 149

Quiet Time and Then Discussion

Questions for Meditation

1. How does severe illness affect the spiritual life of even a strong believer?

2. In what ways does the sacrament of the Anointing of the Sick help us?

3. How should St. Paul's famous saying, "I fill up in my own body that which is lacking in the sufferings of Christ," help the Christian in times of illness?

Prayer

Christ said to his loved ones: "I am with you, fear not, be not anxious." May I, then, be confident, in the trials and crosses of my life, that you, O Lord, will be my constant companion. Whenever I cannot stand, you will carry me lovingly in your arms. May I have no fear of what will happen tomorrow. For the same Eternal Father who cares for me today will take care of me tomorrow and every day of my life. You, O Lord, will either shield me from suffering or give me strength to bear it patiently. May I be at peace, then, and put aside all useless thoughts, anxieties and worries. Amen.

— Terence Cardinal Cooke,
Prayers for Today, 57–58

Meditation Thirty-Four

Viaticum: The Last Sacrament of the Christian

READINGS
John 6:47–58; Catechism *1524–1532*

As death approaches, Anointing of the Sick is administered along with the Eucharist as Viaticum, a word that means food for the journey. Christ comes to us one last time in Holy Communion as we stand on the threshold of eternity. In Viaticum, He is our comfort, our assurance of God's love, our pledge of immortality. When faced with imminent death, it is difficult for most people to see anything other than tragedy and loss. Even Christians can be shaken by the seeming finality of the grave. But as Catholics, we have our Divine Savior, Body, Blood, Soul, and Divinity, with us as we depart this life. His presence enables us to understand and repeat with confidence the famous words of T.S. Eliot: "In my end is my beginning."

Receiving Christ as Viaticum is a prelude to meeting Christ in eternity. As Viaticum, He is our companion as we make the journey; as the Risen Christ, He is the one who greets us at its end. The conclusion of earthly life means the end of everything we have been accustomed to — except the love of God. We can have no comprehension of what the life to come will be like, what existence with God and outside of time will be. All we know is that it will be immeasurably fuller than life as we have known it and that God will keep his promises to us in ways that the human imagination could never begin to comprehend.

Quotation for Meditation

Even in this fallen world, once in a rare while, you attend the death of someone who was completely prepared to go. That's the kind of funeral you could be a bit happy at. I recall the funeral of my dear friend Mother Mary of Jesus of the Sisters of the Blessed Sacrament in Yonkers. She was ninety-four years old and had been in the cloister since 1916. I got permission to go into the cloister to visit her shortly before her death. She was propped up in bed, blind, lame, and beautifully cared for by her religious sisters. I announced my arrival by asking, "Mother, how are you?" She replied, "Well, Father, you know what Benjamin Franklin used to say." (This lady was filled with surprises; how many cloistered nuns quote Benjamin Franklin?) Cautiously I answered,

"Not really." With a twinkle in her blind eyes, she answered with this quotation: "He used to say when he was old, 'I'm still living in the house, but the roof has caved in.'" This was a lady who was ready to go.

— Fr. Benedict J. Groeschel, C.F.R.,
Arise from Darkness, 110–111

◦◦ Quiet Time and Then Discussion ◦◦

Questions for Meditation

1. What is Viaticum and why is it given?
2. Christ's coming to us as Viaticum as we approach earthly death can be seen as what kind of pledge?
3. How should the Catholic Christian face his own mortality?

Prayer

O Lord and Savior,
support me in my last hour
in the strong arms of your sacraments
and by the power of
your consolations.
Let the absolving words be said over me;
and the holy oil sign and seal me.
And let your own Body be my food,
and your Blood my sprinkling.
And let my Mother, Mary, breathe on me.
And my glorious saints and my own
patrons smile upon me that,
in them all and through them all,
I may receive the gift of perseverance,
and die as I desire to live —
in your Church,
in your service,
and in your love. Amen.

— Ven. John Henry Cardinal Newman,
as cited in *Prayers for Today*, 64

The Sacrament of Holy Orders

⟨ornament⟩

READINGS
Exodus 28:1–4 and 29 (entire chapter); John 20:19–23;
Catechism *1533–1538*

In the book of Exodus, God liberates the Jews from slavery and leads them to the Promised Land across scorching expanses of barren wilderness. As they trek through the desert, God performs many signs and wonders, saving His people from death over and over again. At Sinai, amid peals of thunder, He reveals Himself and offers the people a covenant, allowing them to bind themselves to His purpose forever.

And as soon as this covenant is sealed, God directs that a tabernacle be built and a priesthood be established. Even though the Israelites are still homeless, vulnerable wanderers, God gives them priests, showing the priesthood to be an indispensable part of the covenanted relationship, a vital element in the life of His chosen people. God sets Aaron, brother of Moses, apart as the first of a hereditary priestly line who will offer sacrifice to the God of Israel in the name of all. For centuries this priesthood continued to offer their sacrifices. For untold years the temple and the priesthood of the descendants of Aaron were the very heart of the Jewish people's connection to their God.

The Temple in Jerusalem is no more and neither is the priesthood of Aaron and his descendants. Their sacrifices, once so indispensable to the worship of God, have been brought to completion by the one sacrifice of Jesus on the cross, the sacrifice that brings God and man into "a new and unending covenant." As the covenant is made new in Christ, so the priesthood is reborn in Christ as well. Jesus, the one High Priest, calls others to come after Him as he called the Apostles during his earthly life. He graciously offers them a share in the priesthood that by rights belongs to Him alone, a priesthood far deeper than anything Aaron or his descendants could have known. Through this sharing in Christ's priesthood, a man who has received the sacrament of Holy Orders becomes able to open God's inexhaustible storehouse of graces for God's people. Through these sharers in His own divine priesthood, Christ makes unendingly present among us His own sacrifice in the Blessed Sacrament of His Body and Blood.

Holy Orders sets Christ's priests apart like Aaron in the wilds of Sinai. The call to Holy Orders is unique and awesome. It is a call to give up everything and follow Christ, a call to walk in the footsteps of the Apostles, a call be the agent of God's saving graces in a sinful world. To be a priest is to stand *in persona Christi*. The call to priesthood is an indescribable grace and a terrifying responsibility.

Quotation for Meditation

Oh, how great and honorable is the office of priests, to whom it is given to consecrate with sacred words the Lord of majesty; to bless Him with their lips, to hold Him with their hands, to receive Him with their mouths, and to administer Him to others!

Oh, how clean ought those hands to be, how pure that mouth, how holy that body, how unspotted the heart of a priest, into whom the Author of purity so often enters.

From the mouth of a priest nothing but what is holy, no word but what is good and profitable ought to proceed, who so often receives the sacrament of Christ.

— Thomas à Kempis,
The Imitation of Christ, 430–31

≫ Quiet Time and Then Discussion ≪

Questions for Meditation

1. Priesthood is an essential part of what kind of relationship with God?

2. What brought to conclusion the priesthood of the descendants of Aaron?

3. In what way are those in Holy Orders sharers in the one priesthood of Christ?

Prayer

O Jesus, you desire that we pray the Lord of the harvest to send zealous laborers into his harvest. In your mercy raise up in your Church . . . numerous and holy priests, who will take your divine heart as their model and in the exercise of their holy priesthood promote the glory of your heavenly Father and the salvation of those souls whom you have redeemed with your Precious Blood. Amen.

—Terence Cardinal Cooke, *Prayers for Today*, 22

Meditation Thirty-Six

The Priesthood of the Laity

◦❦◦

READINGS
1 Peter 2:4–10; Mark 10:35–45;
Catechism *1539–1553*

S t. Peter, the rock upon whom Christ has built His Church,
teaches us that the entire Body of Christ participates in the
priesthood. In the First Letter of Peter we read: "Come to him,
to that living stone, rejected by men but in God's sight chosen
and precious; and like living stones be yourselves built into a spiritual house, to be a holy priesthood, to offer spiritual sacrifices
acceptable to God through Jesus Christ" (1 Pet 2:4–5). Only a
few lines later Peter reminds the faithful that they are "a royal
priesthood, a holy nation, God's own people, that you may
declare the wonderful deeds of him who called you out of darkness into his marvelous light" (1 Pet 2:9). In this description of
the Church, Peter echoes words from the book of Exodus in

which God says that if the Israelites accept His covenant He will make of them "a kingdom of priests and a holy nation" (Ex 19:6).

Here we encounter a profound truth, that although the priesthood is the special province of those set apart by ordination, it extends in a mysterious way beyond them to include all the baptized. This is acknowledged in the *Catechism* in these words:

> The whole community of believers is . . . priestly. The faithful exercise their baptismal priesthood through their participation, each according to his own vocation, in Christ's mission as priest, prophet and king. Through the sacraments of Baptism and Confirmation the faithful are "consecrated to be . . . a holy priesthood." (CCC 1546)

Since these meditations are read primarily by the laity, it is appropriate while considering the sacrament of Holy Orders to remember the priesthood of the laity, to remind ourselves that by our Baptism we have been given a share of Christ's royal priesthood and been granted a privileged position through God's grace. We, the baptized, have been set apart to serve the Lord. This is our primary responsibility as it is the responsibility of every priest.

Quotation for Meditation

"I appeal to you," [St. Paul] says, "to present your bodies as a living sacrifice." By this exhortation of his, Paul has raised all men to priestly status.

How marvelous is the priesthood of the Christian, for he is both the victim that is offered on his own behalf, and the priest who makes the offering. He does not need to go beyond himself to seek what he is to immolate to God: with himself and in himself he brings the sacrifice he is to offer God for himself. The victim remains and the priest remains, always one and the same. Immolated, the victim still lives: the priest who immolates cannot kill. Truly it is an amazing sacrifice in which a body is offered without being slain and blood is offered without being shed.

— St. Peter Chrysologus, as cited in
Christian Prayer: The Liturgy of the Hours, 1998

Quiet Time and Then Discussion

Questions for Meditation

1. How is the Church a nation of priests, and why is this significant?
2. What are my responsibilities as a sharer in the priesthood of the laity? How do I fulfill them?
3. What is my real understanding of priesthood? Do I take it for granted, or do I see it as the great gift from God that it is?

Prayer

Lord, You have given us unimaginable gifts in Your Word, Your sacraments, and especially in Your Word made flesh, Jesus Christ. Give us, also, we pray, the grace to be Your instruments throughout our earthly life. Let us share Your gifts with all we encounter; let us show by our lives that we serve only You, that we love You, that we give ourselves to others because of You. Make us worthy, Father, to be Your priestly people. We ask this through Christ Our Lord. Amen.

The Threefold Nature of the Sacrament of Holy Orders

⚓

READINGS
Acts 1:8; 2:4; 6:1–6; John 21:15–17;
Catechism *1554–1561*

God is one and exists in indivisible unity. Yet God is three —
Father, Son, and Holy Spirit — and lives in eternal relationship. We have heard this article of our faith repeated so often that we may no longer even see it for the profound mystery that it is; it may have become something of a commonplace to us. We may even think we understand it, but we don't.

The sacrament of Holy Orders is one sacrament, yet it is unique among the sacraments in that it, too, has a threefold nature. In the words of the *Catechism*, "The divinely instituted ecclesiastical ministry is exercised in different degrees by those who even from ancient times have been called bishops, priests, and deacons" (CCC 1554). Those in Holy Orders, whatever their degree, represent Christ to the Church and Christ's Church to the world. Each is transformed at his ordination, bishops and priests (or presbyters) to share in the one high priesthood of Christ, and deacons to serve that high priesthood in every way possible. This ordering is essential to the nature of the Church; it is an indispensable part of God's plan to bring us to Himself in salvation. In the words of St. Ignatius of Antioch, one of the great early Church Fathers, "Let everyone revere the deacons as Jesus Christ, the bishop as the image of the Father, the presbyters as the senate of God and the assembly of the apostles. For without them one cannot speak of the Church" (CCC 1554).

When we encounter a bishop, we encounter one who lives in the absolute fullness of the priesthood. A bishop stands in a direct line of descent from the Apostles. The ordination those twelve frightened, confused men received from Christ at the Last Supper flows down through the ages and remains alive and active in every bishop in the world. The bishop takes the place of Christ Himself in the Church, and it is the bishop's special charge to ordain others as Christ ordained the Apostles. It is through the bishop, and him alone, that God continues to renew the priesthood with new members from generation to generation, from century to century. Bishops in union with the Pope are true and authentic teachers of the faith. As the staff they carry indicates, they are our pastors, our earthly good shepherds. They are, in the words of St. Ignatius of Antioch, "the living image of God the Father" (CCC 1549).

The Twelve Apostles soon became too few in number to shepherd a rapidly growing Church without assistance. In the same way, the bishops cannot care for the multitudes of God's people alone. Through the wisdom of God, sharers in this vital ministry have been provided so that the sacraments and the Word of God will not be withheld from the faithful. Priests are those sharers. They do not have the fullness of the priesthood of Christ — they cannot ordain others — but they act in union with the bishop, and through them Christ comes to us in the Eucharist, our sins are forgiven, and the other sacraments are given to us to bring us to holiness.

In a deacon, one sees Christ in a special way. Christ came to us in humility, putting aside his infinite glory to serve human beings in all their imperfections. His service was without limit; it extended to the very shedding of his blood, the giving of his life on Calvary. As Christ served, so a deacon serves. It is the nature of the diaconal ordination to serve others. The very word "deacon" comes from a Greek word that means service. As a bishop is an icon of the Father, so a deacon can be seen as an icon of Jesus, the suffering servant. In a deacon we see, set apart in a special way by God, that which we must all strive to be.

As God is ultimate mystery, so the priesthood remains shrouded in mystery.

Exactly how those in Holy Orders share in the priesthood of Christ is unknowable to us, but it is sufficient for us to understand that they do, that they are the heart of the Church, that it is through them that Christ has chosen to make Himself present to all.

Quotation for Meditation

"The priest's prayer life in particular needs to be continually 'reformed.' Experience teaches that in prayer one cannot live off of past gains. Every day we need not only to renew our external fidelity to times of prayer, especially to those devoted to the celebration of the Liturgy of the Hours and those left to personal choice and not reinforced by fixed times of liturgical service, but also to strive constantly for the experience of a genuine personal encounter with Jesus, a trusting dialogue with the Father and a deep experience of the Spirit."

— Pope John Paul II, *Pastores Dabo Vobis*
(I Will Give You Shepherds), 194

❧ Quiet Time and Then Discussion ❧

THE THREEFOLD NATURE OF THE
SACRAMENT OF HOLY ORDERS

Questions for Meditation

1. What is the threefold nature of the sacrament of Holy Orders?

2. How is the priesthood of the bishop different from that of the presbyter?

3. Whom should we see in a deacon and why?

Prayer

Almighty Father, we pray for all bishops, priests, and deacons. We ask You to bestow upon them the grace to be worthy ministers of Your Word and sacraments. Grant that they may proclaim Christ with their every word and action. As Your Son is our Divine Shepherd, let them be our faithful earthly shepherds. Make them living symbols of Your love, and give them the grace to walk in the ways of the one High Priest, Jesus, Your Son. Amen.

Meditation Thirty-Eight

The Indelible Character
of the Priesthood

READINGS
Hebrews 5:1–10; 6:13–20; 7 (entire chapter);
Catechism *1581–1589*

For better or worse we are defined by what we do in this world. If we say that so and so is a lawyer or that someone is a teacher, we usually believe we have described these people quite adequately, that we've said all that needs to be said. Our professions often dictate were we stand in society. A doctor has a very different social position than does a car mechanic. Stock brokers live in a different world from the one secretaries occupy. It's as if our professions affect our nature, or perhaps it's more accurate to say: It's as if our professions determine our nature, mark it in some way that cannot easily be changed.

Of course, when we stop to consider it, we realize this cannot possibly be true. We know that we shortchange people when we think of them in this way. We agree that human nature is capable of so many twists and turns that it's not impossible for a store clerk to become a head of state one day or for a well-known actress to end up a waitress. So, what we do is not really what we are — except in the case of the priesthood.

To some, the priesthood may seem to be a profession like any other. But it is not. It is, instead, a mysterious state of being. The priest is not simply someone who is trained to perform certain functions. He is not a professional leader of prayer. He is not just someone who has a gift for ministry, and he is not a religious social worker. A priest is a man who has received the sacrament of Holy Orders. Like all sacraments, this one transforms. It leaves the recipient forever altered. In the words of the *Catechism*, the sacrament of Holy Orders "configures the recipient to Christ . . . so that he may serve as Christ's instrument for his Church. By ordination one is enabled to act as a representative of Christ, Head of the Church, In his triple office of priest, prophet, and king" (CCC 1581). In other words the priest receives an indelible mark at his ordination. He becomes one with what he does. He is not one who performs a priestly ministry. He *is* his priesthood down to the very depths of his innermost being. He can attempt to leave the priesthood, but it will never leave him. He can be prohibited by his ecclesiastical superiors from functioning as a priest, but no one can undo his ordination. He can lose his faith entirely but not his ability to make the Body and Blood of Christ present to us under the forms of bread and wine.

A priest is a priest forever. He is irrevocably marked as being different from the rest of us. Yet he remains a frail, fallible human being. As we have come to know only too well in recent years, he is heir to all the foibles and follies of human nature. Despite his human weakness, however, and irrespective of whether he is saintly or worldly, he remains indissolubly linked to the one High Priest, Jesus Christ. Through that linkage he connects us to the Father, Son, and Holy Spirit in a way that otherwise would not be possible. For that we thank our God every day.

Quotations for Meditation

"We priests are not dispensable functionaries: we are bridges to the very mystery of God and healers of the soul. When we claim this priestly identity unapologetically, we not only find ourselves, we also provide the Church and our culture with the sustenance they require."

— Joseph Cardinal Bernardin, as quoted by Bishop Timothy M. Dolan in *Priests for the Third Millennium*, 229

———

In our Catholic understanding, priestly ordination is a radical, total reordering of a man in the eyes of God and his Church, bringing about an identity of ontological "reconfiguration" with Christ. This priestly identity is at the very core, the essence, of a man, affecting his being and, subsequently, his actions.

— Bishop Timothy M. Dolan,
Priests for the Third Millennium, 229

❧ Quiet Time and Then Discussion ❧

Questions for Meditation

1. When a man receives the sacrament of Holy Orders, how is he transformed?
2. How does the Catholic priesthood differ from the ministry of Protestant bodies?
3. How does the existence of the priesthood demonstrate God's great love for us?

Prayer

O, Jesus, I pray for Your faithful and fervent priests; for Your unfaithful and tepid priests; for Your priests laboring at home and abroad in distant mission fields; for Your tempted priests; for the lonely and desolate priests; for Your young priests; for Your dying priests; for the souls of Your priests in Purgatory. Amen

— From a prayer by Richard Cardinal Cushing,
as cited in the *Vatican II Sunday Missal*

Marriage in God's Plan

⚜

READINGS
Genesis 1:26–28; Matthew 19:6; Revelation 19:7, 9;
Catechism *1601–1620*

So God created man in His own image; in the image of God He created them: male and female He created them. And God blessed them, and God said to them, "Be fruitful and multiply." So reads the first creation account in the book of Genesis. In this beautiful story, the natural world is brought into being through an act of the divine will and countless living creatures are created to dwell in it. God brings a breathtaking world into existence, but He is not satisfied, for this God is Father, Son, and Holy Spirit. He lives not in solitary remoteness but in eternal relationship, eternal love. The love of God is so strong that He implants the divine image in his final creation, thus giving man the ability to love, the desire to live in relationship, the ability to respond to the one who made him. "Be fruitful and multiply," God says, and man is made the partner of God, charged with continuing the creation that God has begun — continuing it through relationship with each other, continuing it though love.

Thus, marriage is unique among the sacraments, having been ordained as part of the natural order of things before the fall of man. We might even say that God wrote marriage into the DNA of mankind. It is also the basic building block of any society: the fundamental relationship upon which all other relationships are built. The desire not to be alone, the impulse to love another, to want to share one's life — one's very being — with another person is basic to human nature. Marriage brings that basic desire back into its intended place in God's plan for mankind. Marriage sanctifies that desire, making it possible for the intimate relationship between a man and a woman to reflect the divine reality. In the holiness of true marriage — in the wholehearted, unselfish love of one spouse for another — we can discern the unfailing love with which God loves mankind; we can see the intimate relationship between Christ and His Church.

Quotation for Meditation

The body reveals the "living soul" that man became when God breathed life into him. It's a witness to the fact that all of creation is a gift. Because of this, the body is a witness to the Love that brings forth and sustains all life. Our masculinity and our femininity — our sex — is the sign of a gift.

By uniting so closely as to become "one flesh," husband and wife open themselves to the blessing of procreation (first spoken of in Genesis 1:28). In Genesis, there is a difference between the sex instinct of animals and the procreative power of human beings. Because man alone is created in the image of God, human sexuality is raised to a higher level — the level of persons.

From the beginning, man's existence as male and female is connected with gift-giving — the nuptial meaning of the body. Human sexuality is fundamentally about mutual self-giving, mirroring the Creator's love.

> — Pope John Paul II, adapted by Sam Torode,
> *Body and Gift, Reflections on Creation*, 30

❧ Quiet Time and Then Discussion ❧

Questions for Meditation
1. In what way is marriage unique among the sacraments?
2. How is marriage the basic building block of society?
3. In what way does marriage enable us to cooperate in God's continuous plan of creation?

Prayer

Father, you have made the bond of marriage a holy mystery,
a symbol of Christ's love for his Church.
Hear our prayers for all married people.
May their lives always bear witness to the reality of that love.
We ask this through our Lord Jesus Christ, your Son,
who lives and reigns with you and the Holy Spirit,
one God, forever and ever. Amen

— From the *Rite of Marriage*

Meditation Forty

The True Nature of Marriage

❧

READINGS
Genesis 2:4–24; Ephesians 5:21–33;
Catechism *1621–1624*

It is hardly a fresh idea to suggest that marriage has fallen onto hard times in our culture. Vast numbers of people enter into marriage with little or no idea of its true nature. Many consider it an arrangement that can be ended for any reason and at any moment. Multiple marriages are the norm, and people spend much of their adult lives acquiring and discarding partners as they restlessly search for — for what? Perhaps they will say they're looking for happiness or a soul mate. As Catholics, we know they're in a desperate search for something deeper, something that will always elude them until they turn from the frantic, shallow, selfish lifestyle the world celebrates and come to understand marriage for what God created it to be. A spouse is not a possession whose value depends on its ability to entertain or satisfy the emotional needs of the moment. A spouse is not an object that can be thrown away when its novelty wears off or when a more interesting toy is discovered. A spouse is a person — the person with whom one shares the deepest relationship possible in this earthly life. A spouse is the person whom one loves without a hint of selfishness. Holy Scripture tells us that when we enter into marriage we are "no longer two but one" (Mt 19:6). Therefore, a spouse is the person we love as we love ourselves, whose life is inextricably bound up with ours, whose happiness is our happiness.

In the world around us, weddings have become circuses — expensive, lavish events that signify nothing. We hear of theme weddings, sports weddings, ski-weekend weddings, beach weddings, costume party weddings, medieval weddings. The list is as sad as it is endless. Marriage needs no theme to be imposed upon it. It has a theme — a forgotten one. It is a sacrament; it is a covenant that reflects Christ's undying love for His Church. At weddings today, vows are often rewritten. "Until death us do part" becomes "As long as love shall last." What kind of love is this that can evaporate like water in the summer sun?

The Church in her wisdom stands firm against all this and preserves Marriage as the sacrament God intended it to be. A Catholic wedding does not take place in a park or a catering hall. It is solemnized at God's altar, before the Blessed Sacrament, usually within the context of the celebration of the Eucharist. This is essential, for it clearly shows the sacramental nature of marriage; it reminds us that marriage is a holy and indispensable part of God's plan for mankind. As the bride and groom receive the Eucharistic Christ during their wedding, their self-giving to each other is linked to His self-giving to all mankind. The covenant of marriage is thus made clear to be an earthly symbol of the covenant between Christ and the Church. In the Church's celebration of marriage we become aware that this sacrament, like all sacraments, has its origin in the Paschal Mystery of Christ, that it flows from the wounded side of Christ, that it is mystical, that it is indissoluble, that it leads us to God.

How can such a theme not be enough for us?

Quotation for Meditation

In the second chapter of John's Gospel, Jesus, Mary, and the disciples are numbered among the invited guests of wedding party. According to the Scripture text, "On the third day there was a wedding feast at Cana in Galilee, and the mother of Jesus was there. Jesus and his disciples were also invited to the wedding" (Jn 2:1–2). The wedding feast was not uneventful. A shortage of wine and a mother's request allowed the opportunity for Jesus to perform his first sign. He transformed ordinary water into exceptional wine. A celebration of marriage thus became a manifestation of God's glory. "Jesus did this at the beginning of his signs in Cana in Galilee and so revealed his glory, and his disciples began to believe in him" (Jn 2:11). Cana was both an event of God's glory and an affirmation of the institution of marriage. According to the *Catechism*, "The Church attaches great importance to Jesus' presence at the wedding at Cana. She sees in it the confirmation of the goodness of marriage and the proclamation that thenceforth marriage will be an efficacious sign of Christ's presence" (CCC 1613). Jesus' support of marriage did not end at Cana.

— Joseph Giandurco and John Bonnici,
Partners in Life and Love, 14–16

Quiet Time and Then Discussion

Questions for Meditation

1. What is the significance of a couple receiving the Eucharist during the marriage celebration?

2. What is the Church's understanding of love within the context of marriage?

3. What is the true relationship between spouses in a sacramental marriage?

Prayer

Almighty God, in whom we live and move and have our being, look graciously upon the world you have made and for which your Son gave his life, and especially on all whom you make to be one flesh in holy marriage. May their lives together be a true sacrament of your love in this broken world, so that unity may overcome estrangement, forgiveness heal guilt, and joy overcome despair.

— After a prayer found in
The Book of Alternative Services

Marriage: An Indissoluble Union of Equals

‿

READINGS
1 John 4;16; John 15:9–12;
Catechism *1638–1642*

The sacrament of Matrimony sanctifies the bond of love between a man and woman. It consecrates them, setting them apart for each other, enabling them to find genuine holiness in each other. In a true marriage, each spouse helps to bring the other to God. At the heart of this great sacrament is a solemn commitment to reflect the divine love, for the married person must love his or her spouse unselfishly as God loves us unselfishly, as Christ loves His bride, the Church. The love found in a true, holy marriage remains unshaken despite a spouse's inevitable failures and inadequacies, just as God's love for each of us remains unshaken despite our endless sinfulness. The love of the Persons of the Holy Trinity for each other is so great that it spills over, bringing a universe into being. In a similar way, the love of a married couple is so great that it joins them to God's inexhaustible creative power. It too spills over and brings new life into being — new life that is in turn capable of love, of holiness, of eternal joy.

Marriage existed before the time of Christ. In fact, marriage in one form or other is a feature of every culture and every time. Often, such marriages had little of the holy about them. Brides were bought; wives and children were but expendable possessions; multiple simultaneous marriages were often the norm. Marriage was sometimes a means of forming an alliance between powerful families, a simple business arrangement. At best, marriage was but a contract like any other contract. As Christ brings redemption to all things that sinful man corrupts, so Christ transforms marriage, making it not a mere type of ownership or a means to power. Christ makes marriage a true and indissoluble union of equals. By suffusing marriage with sacramental grace, Christ suffuses it with genuine love. He transforms it from a human institution, elevating it until it shares in the divine plan of salvation, until it becomes a pathway to the Father.

Quotation for Meditation

A contract can be made where two or more people agree on a course of action, but there the matter may end. Not so with marriage. The marrying partners not only agree to take each other as husband and wife, but also to continue taking each other until death, to begin to live with one another in the most intimate union possible between two people, and to share their respective lives with one another (and whatever children God may send them) by forming a family. If all institutions worthy of the name are established societies — especially those of a public character, which affect the welfare of the community — marriage is not only an institution, it is the basic institution of human society on which all other corporate establishments somehow depend.

— John A. Hardon, S.J., *The Catholic Catechism*, 532

ᴥ Quiet Time and Then Discussion ᴥ

Questions for Meditation

1. In making marriage a sacrament, how does Christ transform it?

2. What is the model for Christian marriage?

3. How do we live out the sacramentality of marriage in our own lives?

Prayer

Heavenly Father, You created us in Your own image and likeness, and re-created us through Grace as Your children. At the same time, You re-created the union of man and woman in sacramental marriage into a living image of the union of Christ with those who are His members, His Body.

Give to those who have entered this common life . . . an awareness of the holiness and strength of their union as they carry the message of Christ's love for His members, and the inseparable bond which His bride, His body, has with Him.

With faith in You and in each other, may their lives bear witness to Your love and theirs, and may their love last like Yours into eternity. Amen.

— Terence Cardinal Cooke, *Prayers for Today*, 31

Meditation Forty-Two

The Sacredness of Conjugal Love

୬୴

READINGS
Song of Songs 8:6–7; Mark 10:1–16;
Catechism *1643–1654*

Conjugal love, true love between a man and a woman, finds its expression and only fulfillment in the sacrament of Matrimony. How could it be otherwise? Such human love is a gift of God and a reflection of the divine love. As such, it is holy. As such, it must be lived in holiness, lived in intimate connection with the divine love, with love at its purest. Any attempt to sever marital love from the source of all love will lessen it, deform it, turn it into something other than what God intended it to be. True conjugal love is total. Like the love of God, it withholds nothing from the beloved. In Matrimony, we joyfully make a gift of ourselves, body and soul, to the one we marry. This commitment is not for the moment or even for a large portion of our lives. It is forever. We give of ourselves and receive the gift of our

226

spouse during every instant of our married lives, just as we receive the love of God for every instant of our lives. It is a constant, a defining feature of our lives. It is one of the things that makes us who we are.

The sacrament of Matrimony is a sacrament of unity. We find this unambiguously proclaimed in the Gospel of St. Mark. Jesus says, "From the beginning of creation, 'God made them male and female.' For this reason a man shall leave his father and mother and be joined to his wife, and the two shall become one. So they are no longer two but one. What, therefore, God has joined together, let not man put asunder" (Mk 10:8–10).

This unity which is found in Marriage has as its pattern the perfect unity that is rooted in God himself. The three persons of the Blessed Trinity live forever in perfect love for each other. They remain forever distinct yet forever one. In this profound mystery we find a model for our married lives. We see that in marriage we surrender our individuality in order to encounter another person at the most basic of levels, at the deepest level of love, yet somehow our individuality is not lost; it is instead enhanced, enriched, renewed, made holy.

Our contemporary culture proclaims marriage to be an agreement between two people, a hermetic relationship, an arrangement that concerns none but the husband and wife. But if marital love is to reflect the love of God, this is impossible.

God is part of every real marriage, the possibility of offspring is also part of every real marriage. True love — love rooted in the love of God — grows until it overflows from the original relationship and includes others. The love found in all true marriages is too strong, too unselfish to be restricted. As we grow in love of God we grow in love for the one to whom we are married. As the married person grows in love of his spouse, he grows in the love of God.

This is God's plan for marriage. This is what makes it the basic human relationship upon which every culture is built. This is why Holy Mother Church honors it and works so tirelessly to preserve and protect it. This is why it is a sacrament and such a great gift from God.

Quotation for Meditation

If we want to know anything about man, first we have to notice that he exists as a dual being, male and female. We have to start with the idea of "communion." Adam and Even were created to live in unity and harmony. And even in our fallen world, this remains God's design for marriage.

"For this reason," says Genesis 2:24, "a man will leave his father and mother and be united to his wife, and they will become one flesh." When is this union realized? Most clearly, it is expressed when a husband and wife unite sexually, in the marriage act — giving their whole selves to each other and opening themselves to the creation of new life. This intimate union, where a man and a woman cling to each other so closely that they become one flesh, is made possible by our creation as male and female.

Every time a husband and wife come together in this way they rediscover the mystery of creation. Looking in each other's eyes, they recognize their common humanity, reenacting in a special way that first meeting of man and woman when Adam declared, "This is now bone of my bones and flesh of my flesh."

— Pope John Paul II, adapted by Sam Torode,
Body and Gift, Reflections on Creation, 21

℀ Quiet Time and Then Discussion ℀

Questions for Meditation

1. In what sense does married love reflect the love of God?
2. In what primary way is the Church's understanding of marriage different from that of our surrounding culture?
3. What is love at its purest?

Prayer

Father, when you created mankind
you willed that man and wife should be one.
Bind all married couples together in loving union;
and make their love fruitful so that they may be living
*   witnesses*
to your divine love in the world.
We ask this through our Lord Jesus Christ, your Son,
who lives and reigns with you and the Holy Spirit,
one God, forever and ever. Amen.

— From the *Rite of Marriage*

Meditation Forty-Three

The Family of God

❧

READINGS
Matthew 7:21–27; Matthew 5:13–16;
Catechism *1655–1666*

The Church has often been called the Family of God, and there is great truth to this statement. The family has its origin in the bond of love between a woman and a man. This bond is a gift of God, one hallowed by the sacrament of Matrimony. The product of this bond, the family, is holy and rests at the very heart of the Church. The Church also has its origin in a bond of love, that of God for mankind. The Church flows from the wounded side of Christ, from the source of limitless love.

Christ sanctifies the family by coming into this world as a member of a family. He lived and died as a son who loved His mother and foster father and who was loved by them. The familial aspect of Christianity was evident from the Church's first days. Early members of the Church were often brought into the faith as a household unit; they become Christians not as individuals but as a family. The *Catechism* says of these early Christian families something we might say today of strongly Catholic families, that they were "islands of Christian life in an unbelieving world" (CCC 1655).

The family was shown to be holy, as an institution through which God works, even before the coming of Christ. In the Hebrew Scriptures God brings the Chosen People into being not as a nation but as a family. God calls Abraham and Sarah to follow him and through the gift of a son makes them progenitors of the people He will call His own. When their descendants are brought to Egypt to escape famine, they go as a family consisting of a father, his twelve sons, and their wives and children. In Egypt, they become a nation, but when God finally calls them from slavery into freedom, they go once again as a family, carrying the bones of their ancestors with them.

In Baptism, we are joined to the family that is the Church. Within this great family we receive the faith into our lives, making it our own. In due time we transmit it to our children. Parents are the primary teachers of their children, so it is within the family setting that we learn what it is to grow in the love of God. In this, too, the Church acknowledges and learns from what God has done throughout history. One of the most famous of the many commandments found in the Torah (the first five books of the Bible), a commandment that to this day is recited daily at every Jewish worship service, is this excerpt from Deuteronomy: "And you shall love the Lord your God with all your heart, and with all your soul, and with all your might. And these words which I command you this day shall be upon your heart; and you shall teach them diligently to your children, and shall talk of them when you sit in your house, and when you walk by the way, and when you lie down, and when you rise" (Deut 6:4–8).

Here we see the transmission of faith in God to be a familial obligation of the highest order. In the New Testament we understand this same obligation to be also an act of love. St. Paul conveys this beautifully to his spiritual son Timothy when he writes, "You then, my son, be strong in the grace that is in Christ Jesus, and what you have heard from me before many witnesses entrust to faithful men who will be able to teach others also" (2 Tim 2:1-2).

In all this we begin to perceive the true nature of family as God intends it. We find our family in the people with whom we are related. We find our family in the Church which has accepted us in Baptism. We find our family in the wider world to whom we go in love to share what we have been given in Christ — we share with our entire human family the divine love.

Quotation for Meditation

The family has a special role to play throughout the life of its members, from birth to death. It is truly "the sanctuary of life: the place in which life — the gift of God — can be properly welcomed and protected against the many attacks to which it is exposed, and can develop in accordance with what constitutes authentic human growth." Consequently the role of the family in building a culture of life is decisive and irreplaceable.

— Pope John Paul II, *The Theology of the Body*, 565

❧ Quiet Time and Then Discussion ❧

Questions for Meditation

1. Whose responsibility is it to teach the faith to the family and one generation to the other?
2. In what sense is the Church a family?
3. Where, and in whom, do we find our true family?

Prayer

Dear Lord, may You touch our hearts and mold our character in such a special way that authentic love will be fashioned among our families and carried out in our everyday lives. Help us to love each other and express that love in ways that reveal that You are our Father. Lord, allow us to make You smile when You look upon us. Help us to be holy and filled with love for the Eucharist, our true food and nourishment. Help our Holy Priests to stand tall and separated from this world as they lead the Church into victory by authentic love expressed in their oneness with You.

Lord, I pray especially for Catholic men to become the priests of their homes, the holy men that Christ shed his Blood for them to be, that they would lead their families into the sunlight of God's presence to overcome the darkness of our society.

— Gerard J. Cleffi,
Director of the Oratory of Divine Love

Notes

[1] John C. Olin, *The Catholic Reformation: Savonarola to Ignatius Loyola* (New York: Harper & Row, 1969), 16.

[2] Cf. *Catherine of Genoa: Purgation and Purgatory, The Spiritual Dialogue*, trans. Serge Hughes; Introduction by Fr. Benedict J. Groeschel (Paulist Press, 1979).

[3] Lincoln Barnett, *The Universe and Dr. Einstein*, 105–106, copyright © 1948 by Harper & Brothers. Copyright © 1948 by Lincoln Barnett. Revised editions copyright © 1950, 1957 by Lincoln Barnett. Reprinted by permission of HarperCollins Publishers.

[4] Cf. John 17:4.

[5] Cf. Luke 1:23; Acts 13:2; Romans 15:16, 27; 2 Corinthians 9:12; Philippians 2:14–17, 25, 30.

[6] Fr. Benedict J. Groeschel, C.F.R., and James Monti, *In the Presence of Our Lord* (Huntington, Indiana: Our Sunday Visitor, 1997), 59.

[7] Rev. James T. O'Connor, *The Hidden Manna* (San Francisco: Ignatius Press), 317–318.

[8] Groeschel and Monti, 178–179.

[9] Hans Urs von Balthasar, *New Elucidations* (San Francisco: Ignatius Press, 1986), 115.

[10] Groeschel and Monti, 80.

[11] Venatius Honorius Fortunatus, trans. by John M. Neale.

Works Cited

In addition to sacred Scripture and excerpts from the *Catechism of the Catholic Church*, the following works are cited in this book.

St. Augustine

Augustine Through the Ages, ed. Allan D. Fitzgerald (Wm. B. Eerdmans Publishing Co., 1999).

The Enchiridion on Faith, Hope, and Love (Henry Regnery Company, 1961).

Sermon 8, *Liturgy of the Hours*, II (Catholic Book Publishing Company, 1975).

St. Basil, Sermon in *The Liturgy of the Hours* (Catholic Book Publishing Company, 1975).

Terence Cardinal Cooke, *Prayers for Today* (Alba House, 1991).

Jean-Pierre de Caussade, S.J., *Abandonment to Divine Providence*, trans. John Beevers (Image-Doubleday, 1975).

St. Francis de Sales, *An Introduction to the Devout Life* (Tan Books and Publishers, 1994).

Timothy M. Dolan, *Priests for the Third Millennium* (Our Sunday Visitor, 2000).

Joseph Giandurco and John Bonnici, *Partners in Life and Love* (Alba House, 1996).

Fr. Benedict J. Groeschel, C.F.R.
  In the Presence of Our Lord (Our Sunday Visitor, 1997).
  The King Crucified and Risen (Servant Publications, 2002).
  Arise from Darkness (Ignatius Press, 1995).

Romano Guardini, *Prayer in Practice* , trans. Prince Leopold of
  Lowenstein-Wertheim copyright © 1957 by Pantheon Books,
  renewed 1985 by Random House, Inc. Used by permission
  of Pantheon Books, a division of Random House, Inc.

St. John Chrysostom, Sermon in *Christian Prayer: The Liturgy of
  the Hours* (Catholic Book Publishing Company, 1975).

John Hardon, S.J., *The Catholic Catechism* (Doubleday, 1981).

Pope John Paul II
  The Spirit, Giver of Life and Love, Volume III, (Pauline Books
    and Media, 1996).
  Walk According to the Spirit (Pauline Books and Media, 1985).
  I Will Give You Shepherds (United States Catholic Confer-
    ence, 1992).
  The Theology of the Body (Pauline Books & Media, 1997).

St. Hilary, Sermon in *Christian Prayer: The Liturgy of the Hours*
  (Catholic Book Publishing Company, 1975).

Thomas à Kempis, *The Imitation of Christ* (Confraternity of the
  Precious Blood, 1982).

Blessed Columba Marmion, *Christ, the Life of the Soul*, trans.
  Alan Bancroft (Zaccheus Press, 2005).

Luis M. Martinez, *True Devotion to the Holy Spirit* (Sophia Institute Press, 2000).

James T. O'Connor, *The Hidden Manna* (Ignatius Press, 1988).

The Oxford Book of Prayer, ed. George Appleton (Oxford University Press, 1985).

St. Peter Chrysologus, Sermon in *Christian Prayer: The Liturgy of the Hours* (Catholic Book Publishing Company, 1975).

St. Thomas Aquinas, in *Christian Prayer: The Liturgy of the Hours*, (Catholic Book Publishing Company, 1975).

Sam Torode, *Body and Gift* (Philokalia Books, 2003).

The Twentieth Century Encyclopedia of Catholicism, ed. Henri Daniel-Rops; ed. English Language Edition, Lancelot C. Sheppard (Hawthorn Books, 1964).

The Vatican II Sunday Missal (The Daughters of Saint Paul, 1974).

Papal documents not cited above are taken from the Vatican website, www.vatican.va.

Contact Information

Oratory of Divine Love

For further information about the Oratory of Divine Love, go to their website, www.oratorydl.com, or write to:

Oratory of Divine Love
P. O. Box 1465
Bloomfield, NJ 07003

Franciscan Friars and Sisters of the Renewal

Contributions for the work of the Franciscan Friars and Sisters of the Renewal may be sent to:

Padre Pio Shelter
Fr. Benedict J. Groeschel, C.F.R.
Box 55
Larchmont, NY 10538